THE LOGIC OF DEMOCRACY

THE LOGIC OF DEMOCRACY

Thomas Landon Thorson

THE UNIVERSITY OF WISCONSIN

HOLT, RINEHART AND WINSTON
New York · Chicago · San Francisco
Toronto · London

LIBRARY OF CONGRESS CATALOG CARD NUMBER: 62–8423
03–010965–5
PRINTED IN THE UNITED STATES OF AMERICA
90123 4 987

For Ray Addington
and Byrum Carter

PREFACE

This is another book about the intellectual plight of modern man. Many have preceded it, and there are sure to be many to follow. In an important sense, however, what I have written differs sharply from most of the literature which bears upon this subject. I have not stepped back and unleashed a scattered blast in the general direction of thinking humanity in the twentieth century. My weapon is not a shotgun, but a rifle—I hope a moderately high-powered one. The target is quite a specific one, but the haze which surrounds it makes it difficult to take aim and perhaps even more difficult to hit.

The subject with which I try to deal is political values; more specifically, democracy as a political value. In one way this is the question in the center of day-to-day contemporary politics. It is no secret that modern men are in the midst of an ideological conflict; a struggle to choose between democratic institutions and authoritarian ones. It is perhaps something more of a secret, but not much more, that all is not well in this struggle so far as democrats are concerned. We have only to recall President Eisenhower's famous press conference comment that he was "hard put" to defend our system against the arguments of his wartime comrade Marshall Zhukov to know that things are not altogether healthy. Americans have felt compelled to fight the "ideological" struggle with prefabricated houses and shiny kitchens. A good deal can be said for prefabricated houses and shiny kitchens, but it seems evident that they are not "ideological" weapons. My question, I think, is the genuine ideological question. "Why are democratic political principles to be preferred over authoritarian ones?" To put it more technically, as I think we must, "Is there a rational justification for democracy, and if so, what is it?"

At the risk of being accused of snobbery, it must be said that at the level of emotion and propaganda this is a problem for all men, but basically it is a problem for intellectuals. Anyone who recognizes a philosophical question when he sees one knows that political disputes, if they are pushed very far at all, become philosophical disputes. The thrashing out of ultimate political choices, while in a very real sense the concern of all men, is the social function of political philosophy. This is why John Locke and Karl Marx are important people. Unfortunate though it may be, political philosophy is a rather technical and exacting subject. It would perhaps be pleasant if we could handle the problem of justifying democracy in an easier way, but I am afraid that we cannot. The reader is likely to find what follows somewhat demanding. I think, however, that he will not find it obscure.

American society, like societies before it, but perhaps even more so, has delegated the task of thinking seriously about politics to professionals. Of course, it would be possible and perhaps even fruitful to deal with democracy—the political value—as a sociological problem. We could under this sort of scheme probe the attitudes toward democracy of such people as newspaper editors, political orators, Rotarians, trade unionists, farmers, boy scouts. I have chosen to deal, however, not with the sociological problem, but with the intellectual problem. I concentrate therefore on the professional custodians of political values, the political scientists and the philosophers. My problem is first and foremost the justification of democracy, but it is also the analysis and criticism of the handling of the problem of justifying democracy by the professionals.

It is an exceedingly rare event in the modern world for a professional political scientist to attempt to present systematically a justification for a political system. That this is so rare is symptomatic of modern man's intellectual problem in this area. The great success and consequent prestige of the methods of natural science has pushed aside the justification of political systems. Scholars interested in political values, frightened by the strictures of the scientists and their emulators, retreat to textual analysis of the classics, either philosophical or theological. Students of contemporary political affairs, grasping for scientific respectability, exclude questions of value altogether or at least profess to do so. Only a few religious thinkers, most notably the Roman Catholics, are actively philosophizing about politics today and they rely largely on notions which are at least five hundred years old. Thus a dilemma apparently presents itself to professional students of politics—*either* we justify political systems *or* we are scientific, but not both. This is a specific aspect of the general modern problem of moral man in a scientific world, and I have done what I can to explore it and to suggest a possible solution.

I am painfully aware of my inadequacies. My highest hope is that this essay will provoke, that it will stimulate the reader to rethink problems which he may have pushed to the back of his consciousness. My only request is that it be read from beginning to end, for its significance, if indeed it has any, will be missed if it is not read carefully. I would especially advise against attempting to get the substance of the argument by reading only the conclusions in the final chapters; for these conclusions stand upon the foundation which goes before.

My debts are legion and I can acknowledge only the most prominent of them. To political scientists Byrum E. Carter and Charles S. Hyneman of Indiana University; Alpheus T. Mason, Harold Sprout, and William Ebenstein of Princeton University; Charles Anderson of The University of Wisconsin; and my friends Wayne A. Kimmel and Charles H. McCall now of Yale University goes my gratitude for help of the widest variety. For an intellectual experience which I shall probably never fully appreciate, my thanks go to Henry B. Veatch, Norwood Russell Hanson, David Bidney, and Newton P. Stallknecht of the Department of Philosophy, Indiana University.

Three special acknowledgments are in order. The public schools of LaPorte, Indiana, and Indiana University deserve and have my most profound gratitude for encouragement both intellectual and financial. To philosopher James Ward Smith of Princeton University, whose remarkable book *Theme for Reason* informed and stimulated much of what I have said here, go my thanks and admiration. Finally, thanks go to my wife and to my mother and father for help which I cannot adequately describe. I need not say that I alone am responsible for what I have written.

Thomas Landon Thorson

Madison, Wisconsin
January, 1962

CONTENTS

*A person caught in a philosoph-
ical confusion is like a man in a
room who wants to get out but
doesn't know how. He tries the
window but it is too high. He tries
the chimney but it is too narrow.
And if he would only* turn around,
*he would see that the door has been
open all the time!*
                                        Wittgenstein

1

INTRODUCTION

DIRECTION: A JUSTIFICATION FOR DEMOCRACY

Anyone who undertakes the writing of an essay on democracy is obliged to make clear from the outset the way in which he plans to approach this vast and complicated subject. It is perhaps not even necessary to mention the multitude of connotations and denotations that this remarkable term carries. As Professor Laski once remarked, "No definition of democracy can adequately comprise the vast history which the concept connotes."[1] No doubt an interesting and fruitful study could be done in the lexicography of democracy, choosing either all recorded history as the area of research or simply the contemporary uses to which the term is put. I shall not, however, be primarily concerned with this enterprise, even though what I shall ultimately have to say might in some sense be considered an essay in definition.

It is common practice among present-day writers about democracy, especially those who are academically denominated "political scientists," to posit a set of criteria that are to be taken as constituting an objective or scientific model of democracy.[2] Democratic theory formulated within this scheme is concerned with investigating the logical implications of the model, the way in which a government so organized does in fact work, the way in which a government can best implement the model, or some combination of the three. This procedure is employed, as economist Anthony Downs suggests, in order "to avoid ethical premises." The inclination of these students of politics is to sharply differentiate political science from ethics, and thus political theory from moral philosophy. Will-

1

moore Kendall argues that "political theory is itself value-free"[3] as distinguished from ethics or theology. To be sure, Locke, St. Thomas, or Plato would not have agreed; rather, they would have assented to the contrary proposition that political theory is "value-impregnated" (to borrow a term from R. M. MacIver that is not, strictly speaking, appropriate).

The notion of a value-free social science and thus of a value-free political theory is not, however, without good grounds. It flows from modern philosophical developments that flow in turn from modern scientific developments. This is the philosophical point of view ordinarily designated, for want of a more appropriate general term, "logical positivism."[4] David Easton expresses this point of view in the following way:[5]

> To avoid any possible doubt that may arise later, however, I must dwell for a moment on my working assumption about the properties of a value judgment, an assumption which has informed and will continue to prevail in the present work. This assumption, generally adopted today in the social sciences, holds that values can ultimately be reduced to emotional responses conditioned by the individual's total life-experiences. In this interpretation, although in practice no one proposition need express either a pure fact or a pure value, facts and values are logically heterogeneous. The factual aspect of a proposition refers to a fact of reality; hence it can be tested by reference to the facts. In this way we check its truth. The moral aspect of a proposition, however, expresses only the emotional response of an individual to a state of real or presumed facts. It indicates whether and the extent to which an individual desires a particular state of affairs to exist. Although we can say that the aspect of a proposition referring to a fact can be true or false, it is meaningless to characterize the value aspect of a proposition in this way.

This point of view need not be evaluated at present, although eventually it will have to be weighed seriously. What must be grasped now, however, is the way in which this conception of values leads to the notion of a value-free social science and thus to a purely instrumental conception of democratic theory. Conveniently, Easton himself applies these standards in talking about democracy:[6]

Let us assume that we agree that democracy is a political system in which power is so distributed that control over the authoritative allocation of values lies in the hands of the mass of the people. To say that "the United States is a democracy," can obviously be proved or disproved, given accessibility to appropriate data. We can speak of the truth or falsity of such a proposition. But to say, "I prefer democracy," introduces a proposition with a logically different aspect. It expresses my sentiment in favor of this kind of political system. We can say that it is true or false that I hold this kind of sentiment, or that it is incompatible with an equal preference for an authoritarian political system, or that, to be consistent, I ought not to give my political support to a movement that would destroy democracy. To assert that this value judgment is true makes sense in another way as well; namely, that it is true that I made the statement or that it expresses the sentiment that I felt and is not an attempt at deception about my emotions. *But it has little meaning to say that my preference for democracy is true while someone else's dislike of it is false.*

The significance here, of course, is that from this point of view there is no proving that democracy is "good" or that it is "better" than fascism or communism, just as there is no proving any value judgment. A proposition such as "Majority rule is the best decision-making procedure for a society" within the framework of this analysis becomes equivalent to shouting "Majority rule!" in the same tone of voice that one might use for "Hurrah!" at a football game.[7] What the democratic theorist must therefore do is to posit political equality, majority rule, and minority rights as simply given and make the business of democratic theory purely instrumental, that is, calculate the implications of the "givens" and discover the most efficient ways of implementing them.

Now it would be naïve and misleading to suppose that all writers on democracy adhere to this position, or that those who do as a matter of fact make no distinction or choice between majority rule and despotism. This viewpoint has been presented in an excessively brief and somewhat heavy-handed way in order to cast in sharp relief the chief point of interest of this essay. I shall not be interested in instrumental democratic theory; instead, I propose to examine the justification for the essential principles of democracy themselves. In this discussion political equality, majority rule, or minority rights will not be posited as given, but an attempt will be made to find the grounds on which these principles may be justified.

Such a proposal is, of course, very much out of fashion in contemporary writing about democracy. It is in fact quite likely to be met with a smile of disbelief. My friend and former teacher Professor Charles S. Hyneman would surely say he can now predict that I will retreat to the nearest closet and begin to pray. Other reactions will surely be similar, although perhaps less graphic. We intend to look for the "foundations" of democracy, even though we are told by philosopher T. D. Weldon " . . . that no such foundations exist and . . . all attempts to demonstrate the superiority of the foundations on which democracy rests to those of communism and totalitarianism are pointless."[8] We are going to search for a philosophy of democracy, even after being told that this is a dangerous, if not immoral, enterprise. Historian Daniel J. Boorstin is among the most vociferous critics of the notion of a philosophy of democracy:[9]

> Some Americans, however—and they are probably increasing in number—make the un-American demand for a philosophy of democracy. They believe that this philosophy will be a weapon against Russia and a prop for our own institutions. They are afraid that, without some such salable commodity, they may not be able to compete with Russia in the world market.
>
> These people are puzzled that we should have come as far as we have without knowing the philosophy which lies beneath our institutions. They are even frightened at what they might find—or fail to find—when they open the *sanctum sanctorum* of national belief. It is these who are among our most dangerous friends; for, even if they should find the Holy of Holies empty, they would refuse to admit it. Instead of trying to discover the reasons why we have managed to be free of idolatry, they will make their own graven image, their own ass's head, and say that is what belonged in the temple all the time. These people are dangerous because they would misrepresent us abroad and corrupt us at home.

There is no need to be frightened by these statements, provided that we understand what they mean. Weldon is right when he says that the *kinds* of foundations he is talking about are illusory, but this does not mean that there are no foundations. Boorstin is right when he says that the builders of "graven images" are dangerous, but this does not mean that *all* philosophers *build* graven images or that there is no philosophy of democracy. In other words, we shall agree with Weldon and Boorstin in "throwing out the dirty bath water," but we shall object when the baby is thrown out as well.

FOCUS: DEMOCRACY AS A PHILOSOPHICAL PROBLEM

I have suggested that we shall discuss certain principles which are central to what we know as democracy. These have been tentatively enumerated as political equality, majority rule, and minority rights. Moreover, I have said that we shall talk about the justification of these principles and not about how they work. It is advisable at this early stage to clarify this distinction and, in addition, to make clear why it should be made and why one aspect will be chosen as the point of interest rather than the other.

These points can perhaps best be made by discussing certain problems raised by the principle of majority rule. Obviously, the principle of majority rule is a concept that will *have* to be justified if our putative justification for democracy is to make any sense; yet reflection on majority rule reveals a host of problems. There is, of course, a certain primary sense in which we all understand what is meant by majority rule. When, for example, the United States Senate passes a bill by a vote of 51 to 49, no one taking the vote at face value would doubt that this is an instance of majority rule. In other words, all would agree that whenever a minimum of 50 per cent plus 1 can make a decision for the entire body, "majority rule" is a proper description of that body's decision-making procedure. However, when we hear that the Senate passed a bill 40 to 39, or that only 40 per cent of the eligible voters in a certain constituency did in fact vote in a particular election, or that the "eligible" voters make up only 60 per cent of the actual population, we begin to worry about what the principle of majority rule really means.

We may simply want to justify rule by the majority as opposed to rule by one or by a few. This appraisal, I think, is essentially correct; but even this contention is not without serious difficulties. We now seem to be classifying forms of government as the ancient Greeks did. "To the ordinary Greek it seemed clear that there were three main types of government. There was autocracy or monarchy, government by a single ruler, who might or might not be called a king. There was oligarchy, government by a few specified people, which might sometimes be called aristocracy, if it was intended to claim that the few were also the best. And, finally, there was democracy, government by the whole people or the great majority of them."[10] Again, there is little difficulty in understanding this distinction. It means something, and what is more, it means something significant. However, if the myriad acts and decisions that make up the day-to-day business of a modern government are under consideration, difficulties immediately come into view. "If we consider all the complications involved in this matter of taking decisions, we shall see that it would be extremely difficult to imagine a state in which *all* the decisions were taken either by a single autocrat or by the whole body of citizens" or, for that matter, by "a selected few."[11]

Thus, if the workings of modern "democratic" states are subjected to close scrutiny, all three of these elements will surely be found operating in the decision-making process.[12]

We can probably conclude with G. C. Field that "in terms of the simple Greek definition every state is a mixture, in varying degrees, of monarchy, oligarchy, and democracy,"[13] and with Robert A. Dahl that democracy in America is really a matter of "minorities rule."[14] How then are we to talk about "justifying" majority rule when we discover that it never in fact operates in a pure form in any context which we find important, that is, in the decision-making procedures of nation-states? Let us lay these difficulties and complications aside for the present. It is, however, important that we recognize the problems before we dispose of them, for there is no defining them out of existence; but it is quite necessary that we *do* dispose of them.

Suppose that we were to take on the task of "justifying," in some philosophical sense, majority rule as it operates in the United States. In the first place, from a practical point of view the task would be difficult, if not impossible; moreover, it would be plain nonsense. Imagine trying to conjure up some kind of ultimate justification for the compromise product of a complex political process—the Connecticut Compromise, the apportionment of Congressional seats in the state of New York, or the party-column ballot. We would, however, need to do just this if we were to talk about majority rule as it operates in the real world. Clearly, therefore, we shall talk about the justification of majority rule in *principle*, and these considerations will be related only tangentially to majority rule in practice. We can perhaps best see the point here by referring again to the model democracies constructed by democratic theorists. Professors Austin Ranney and Willmoore Kendall speak of their model democracy in the following terms:[15]

> Certainly we do not propose to compare all existing governments with our model of democracy and then label "democratic" all those governments that measure up to it in every respect, and lump together all those that do not as "undemocratic." If this were our purpose, we should have great difficulty in finding an acceptable candi-

date for the democratic category, and even some difficulty in discovering a completely eligible candidate for the "undemocratic" category.

*Our model of democracy will serve rather to fix one end of a spec-
trum or scale, along which we can place various existing institutions
and governments.*

We shall thus be focusing on this democratic end of the spec-
trum and shall be attempting to *justify* these democratic principles which the instrumental, "value free" theorists simply
posit as given. While "the majority" may never in fact rule in
any given situation, in a democracy the majority principle is
the rule under which coalitions form and in terms of which
minorities rule.

A choice of distributing emphasis in one way rather than
another has been made, but can we be sure that the choice is a
legitimate or a wise one? It might be argued that there is little
purpose in thrashing around in the somewhat nebulous area
of justification since most people agree democracy is desirable
anyway. From this viewpoint, we might better spend our time
worrying about how majority rule is to be implemented or
just how minority rights can be protected. Such a line of argument, however, is not persuasive for at least two reasons. First,
while there is surely room for fruitful examination of varying approaches, say, to majority rule (e.g., proportional representation or single-member constituencies), without a careful examination of the premises on which the principle itself
rests how can we make intelligent choices among various
methods? In other words, if the principles of democracy themselves are not thoroughly investigated, there can be no very
satisfactory standard for putting them into practice. The great
difficulty that has long faced our courts in civil liberties and
property rights decisions is surely ample testimony to this
need. A general feeling of good will toward something called
"democracy" does not help much in assigning limits to free
speech. A close examination of the grounds for the principles
of democracy may not make the task easy, but this is no good

reason to ignore the question. Presumably one of the important things we want to do in setting limits on free speech or in choosing between proportional representation and single-member constituencies is to assign the most "democratic" limits or to make the more "democratic" choice. In order to accomplish this task we must know what the term "democratic" *really* means. By examining the logic of democracy—by justifying it—we shall also in a sense be defining it; that is, we shall be setting up a standard of democracy in terms of which particular procedures can be judged. What meaning a particular judge attaches to the term "democratic" may have a great effect on where he sets the limits to free speech. Surely it is not inaccurate to view the difference between the Supreme Court majority and Mr. Justice Douglas in dissent in a case such as *Dennis et al. v. United States* as a matter of differing conceptions of democracy.

In 1942, W. T. Stace stated a second and, I should say, more important reason for rejecting this argument. He began with a statement of the argument itself:[16]

> Almost all the political controversies which are argued in newspapers, in magazines, on platforms, and even in treatises on political science are concerned not with ends but only with means, not with ultimate goals of political action but only with the machinery for their attainment. This is because the ends or ultimate ideals are generally agreed upon, are taken to be axioms which are common to all parties. . . . Even if the professors of political science should argue in their textbooks such questions as whether it is better to have a written constitution, as in the United States, or no written constitution, as in Britain; whether the chief executive of the state should remain in office for a fixed term of years or resign when he no longer retains a majority of the votes of the people's representatives; whether it is better that judges should be elected or appointed; whether proportional representation would improve our constitution; even these questions, comparatively remote and academic as they may appear to most people, are still concerned only with subordinate questions of machinery.

A hundred other items could probably be added to Stace's already imposing list, and no one would argue that these were unimportant questions. In certain contexts they might be of primary importance. But are the important questions facing us today simply whether we should have democracy in this way or that, or rather are they about whether we should have democracy *at all?* If the fundamental decision to have democracy is itself challenged, as it surely is today, how are we then to argue our case?

Surely, we have no desire to turn this discussion into a propaganda tract, but we can and must recognize the importance of this prior question; and it is undoubtedly a mistake to leave it to the propagandists, excluding it on principle from serious investigation. What we, as students of politics, must come to see is that while the workings of all governments are extraordinarily complex and challenging and while we are not able in the real world to set up any facile dichotomy between democracy and totalitarianism, there is nonetheless a fundamental choice, a basic distribution of emphasis, that simply cannot be excluded from serious consideration. If in practice, as Field puts it, "democracy, like the other forms of government, is . . . a matter of degree, and the possible variations of degree are almost infinite,"[17] we must recognize that these differences of degree between democracy and totalitarianism are not *un*important but *all* important.

We can expect two typical responses to this friendly exhortation. The first would probably go something like this: "I certainly agree that it is important to distinguish between democracy and totalitarianism at the philosophical level. I agree also that it is important to justify democracy in an ultimate sense. But what I don't see is what you're so excited about. The job has already been done by Christianity and classical political philosophy. I admit that we're having some trouble with these 'positivists,' but this will all pass in time. When you understand the universe through the teachings of theology and metaphysics, you will see that democracy follows from them."

The second response will probably take a line something like this: "Well, I can see why this worries you, but I'm a political scientist not a magician. Statements like 'majority rule is good' can't be verified empirically. While I happen to agree that majority rule is good, it's just my opinion and I have no evidence unless you want to say that a lot of people like it or that it has worked pretty well. I'd like to help, but I'm afraid that I can't put my heart into this 'justification' hocus-pocus."[18]

We are, thus, apparently caught on the horns of an insoluble dilemma. People in the first camp purport to have a justification for democracy, but we shall show that their justification will not hold water on logico-philosophical grounds. The second camp agrees that this alleged justification is unsound and then goes on to argue that any justification at all is impossible. We shall accept neither of these positions and spend a good deal of time showing why. In other words, we shall try to show that what has long been thought of as a necessary choice between mutually exclusive alternatives is really a false choice. We have imagined that we must adopt one of two views, each of which is necessarily made up of two factors. On the one hand, the possibility of justification must be accompanied by some kind of metaphysical apparatus. On the other, the acceptance of logico-scientific standards and methods (which deny the validity of any metaphysical apparatus) must be accompanied by the impossibility of any justification. In simple terms, we shall strive to combine the acceptance of logico-scientific standards and methods with justification.

Consequently, we shall be trying to deal with what has been called "the tragedy of twentieth-century political science"[19]— this apparent inability to justify democracy as opposed to the various forms of totalitarianism. While scientific method in the study of politics has borne and will surely continue to bear much fruit, it has brought in its wake a problem so fundamental and a difficulty so profound as to constitute a genuine crisis within political science itself. All too often, however, the true nature of the crisis has been misunderstood in the name

of metaphysics or simply ignored in the name of science.
Professor Brecht makes the point in this way:[20]

> When asked what he regards as the crisis of scientific theory in the
> field of politics within the twentieth century the average student is
> likely to point to the antithesis between democracy and totalitarian-
> ism. This answer would be quite correct if at the time when totali-
> tarian doctrines arose, Western scientific theory had supported the
> democratic value system to the exclusion of others. Actually, however
> . . . this was no longer the case. While most scholars who lived under
> constitutionally limited forms of government were most happy to do
> so, the superiority of the ultimate democratic values over contra-
> dictory standards was no longer supported by them *qua* scientists, and
> could not be under the rules of the scientific method as now under-
> stood. The democratic system of values like all others had become,
> scientifically speaking, merely a "dogma," an "ideology," or . . . a
> "myth." Whoever claimed *scientific* authority for his value system—
> even for democracy—was scientifically *in error*. . . . The real crisis
> in Western *scientific theory*, therefore, is not to be sought in the
> emergence of different ideologies, but in what preceded this event
> by about two decades—the rise of the theoretical opinion that no
> scientific choice between ultimate values can be made.

This, then, is the problem—as put in rather terse form—
being able to accept scientific standards and being able to
"justify" at the same time. At this juncture it is clear that
the road we shall have to travel along will be a tortuous one.
Prudence dictates that we pause at various places along the
way to get our bearings and to make sure that we know where
we are before taking the next step. This is a good spot for the
first "time-out." We began by defining a point of interest, that
of justifying the principles of democracy. Then we tried to
show the necessity of divorcing principle from practice for the
purposes of analysis and in addition tried to show that our
analysis would not suffer from this separation, because one of
the most important characteristics of real societies is that they
tend toward one principle or another. The needs (1) of a
standard of judgment for democratic practice and (2) for an
answer to the totalitarian challenge were acknowledged as
good reasons for choosing this point of interest. We noted the

approaches of metaphysics and science to the problem of justification and implied that these were not the only alternatives.
We examined the approach of science further and tried to
show the profound crisis that scientific method has apparently brought to political science.

METHOD: POLITICAL PHILOSOPHY
AS ACTIVITY

Clearly, we have before us a problem whose importance is
largely social and political; but what can we say of the *nature*
of its *solution?* What is involved in justifying democracy? We
are going to say more than that democracy seems to work or
that many people seem to prefer it. We want to show that it is
somehow "correct," "reasonable," and "logical." This kind of
argument must be more than a complicated way of reinforcing
or rationalizing an emotional predilection. Its perfection
would be an ability to convince anyone with an open mind.

We need to be clear about the particular kind of argument
that this will be. Bertrand Russell asks, "Is there any knowledge in the world which is so certain that no reasonable man
could doubt it?" Clearly, this is just the kind of "knowledge"
we want about democracy. This is philosophical knowledge,
for as Russell says, "philosophy is merely the attempt to answer such ultimate questions, not carelessly and dogmatically,
as we do in ordinary life and even in the sciences, but critically,
after exploring all that makes such questions puzzling, and
after realizing all the vagueness and confusion that underlie
our ordinary ideas."[21] Since, therefore, we are by philosophical
methods seeking philosophical understanding of a problem
relevant to politics, our enterprise might be called "political
philosophy."

These preliminary conclusions may seem rather obvious,
and one may wonder why I came to them in such a circuitous

way. The reason is simply that "political philosophy," as the term is ordinarily used, carries connotations and implications I want intentionally to exclude from our use of the term in conducting the present investigation. We sometimes use the term when all we really mean is something like "point of view about governmental policy," as when someone talks about the "political philosophy of Herbert Hoover." I would be very happy if this usage were totally expunged from the language and if people would say "point of view" or "policy orientation" when this is what they mean.

Although this use of the term may be irritating, it is not the usage that is really troublesome. To the technically inclined student of political thought, "political philosophy" is likely to call up a vision of a grand metaphysic from which political proposals are inferred or deduced. In this sense, Plato is the paradigm for political philosophy. There is, of course, nothing illegitimate about this use; our quarrel with it is simply that it does not accurately describe what we shall be pursuing in this inquiry. What I intend by calling this essay an exercise in political philosophy is merely that we shall be dealing with a problem relevant to politics by philosophical methods. No great *Weltanschauungen* or philosophical anthropologies will be postulated, and no political prescriptions will be deduced from them. Rather, as the British philosophers like to say, we shall be "doing philosophy." Philosophy will be viewed not as a proclamation of truth but as an activity.

Political philosophy then will signify the activity of philosophical analysis directed to questions relevant to politics. We would perhaps do well to say a few words about this sort of political philosophy. There is no book, so far as I am aware, that will serve as a definitive example of this application of the term. We can, however, get some notion by looking briefly at developments within philosophy itself. "The last thirty years or so have witnessed a slow and silent revolution in philosophy which has gone almost unnoticed by the layman,"[22] we are told by the Harvard philosopher Morton White. This revolution consists in the rise of what is sometimes called "analytical" philosophy; in fact, White chose the title *The Age of Analysis*[23] to describe it. While the word "philosopher" was regarded in the past and even today in the popular mind as equivalent to "sage" or "speaker of wisdom," philosophy has in large part become a technical discipline specializing in logic, epistemology, philosophy of science, and a brand of ethics that traditional moralists would have great difficulty recognizing.

The "fat, two-volumed *Weltanschauung*" has on the whole become a thing of the past. This new analytical philosophy is much more intricate and much "tighter," perhaps even to the extent that most of its "finely ground axes have been used to sharpen other axes."[24]

> The temper and tone of the movement is deflationary and critical; its method linguistic and logical. While some of its sponsors emphasize the importance of reconstructing ordinary language, others insist on the need for describing the behavior of words as ordinarily used. What they all oppose, however, is the pretentious method of those who claim to conduct us to the Truth by way of labyrinthine metaphysical systems, aided by the flimsiest threads.

This is no small achievement, for without this movement which can trace its ancestry back to Locke and Hume we might still be looking for answers in a "brooding omnipresence in the sky," as Justice Holmes put it.

We are seeing here a parallel to or, perhaps more accurately, another aspect of a development previously noted in the study of politics. Political scientists, having become convinced of the unscientific character of value statements, feel compelled to push them aside or to posit them as merely given. Philosophers, who might have stepped into the breach, feel the same compulsion. The "loss of touch with cultural and political questions is one of the most striking features of Anglo-American philosophy in the last generation and it constitutes one of the most unfortunate concomitants of a brilliant period in the history of philosophy."[25]

White suggests that the philosophical analyst "dig his honest and sharp instruments" into the subject matter of politics, but he sees that the skillful logician will not accomplish very much just by diving in. "Of course the enormous growth of our knowledge about society and politics since the days of Locke and Mill will make it impossible for a philosopher to go it alone. He will need training in history and the social sciences like that which a philosopher of physics must have in physics."[26] I could not agree more, but I suggest that there is at least one more way of meeting this urgent need. If philosophers can learn about politics, why cannot political scientists learn about philosophy?

Although some philosophers will surely feel that this suggestion is extraordinarily presumptuous, can we be sure that Locke, Plato, Mill, and even Hume were philosophers first and political thinkers second? In any case there is a need to transcend academic boundaries, recognized by some on both sides, and this requires experience in both areas no matter what professional association one belongs to. But it is not enough to plead for an analytical approach to political philosophy, regardless of who is doing the pleading. A political problem must be selected, and some understanding of both politics and philosophy must be applied to it. Presenting reasons for supporting democracy is just such a problem.

NOTES

1 Harold J. Laski, "Democracy," in *Encyclopedia of the Social Sciences,* vol. V (London: Macmillan & Co., Ltd., 1934), p. 76. See also Arne Naess, and associates Jens A. Christophersen and Kjell Kvalø, *Democracy, Ideology, and Objectivity* (Oslo: Oslo University Press, 1956), for a detailed treatment of the modern meanings of democracy.

2 For example, an economist, Anthony Downs, *An Economic Theory of Democracy* (New York: Harper & Brothers, 1957), pp. 23–24:

"To avoid ethical premises, we define democratic government descriptively, i.e., by enumerating certain characteristics which in practice distinguish this form of government from others. A government is democratic if it exists in a society where the following conditions prevail:

1. A single party (or coalition of parties) is chosen by popular election to run the governing apparatus.

2. Such elections are held within periodic intervals, the duration of which cannot be altered by the party in power acting alone.

3. All adults who are permanent residents of the society, are sane, and abide by the laws of the land are eligible to vote in each such election.

4. Each voter may cast one and only one vote in each election.

5. Any party (or coalition) receiving the support of a majority of those voting is entitled to take over the powers of government until the next election.

6. The losing parties in an election never try by force or any illegal means to prevent the winning party (or parties) from taking office.

7. The party in power never attempts to restrict the political activity of any citizens or other parties as long as they make no attempt to overthrow the government by force.

8. There are two or more parties competing for control of the governing apparatus in every election."

See also Robert A. Dahl, *A Preface to Democratic Theory,* copyright 1956 by the University of Chicago (Chicago: University of Chicago Press), and Austin Ranney and Willmoore Kendall, *Democracy and the American Party System* (New York: Harcourt, Brace & World, Inc., 1956), chaps. 1–4.

3 Willmoore Kendall, "Prolegomena to Any Future Work on Majority Rule," *The Journal of Politics,* vol. XII (January, 1950), p. 707.

4 Exacting historians of philosophy are likely to use this term in a much narrower way. Arnold Brecht proposes the term "scientific value relativism" or "scientific value alternativism," which while more precise is less familiar. Arnold Brecht, *Political Theory: The Foundations of Twentieth Century Political Thought* (Princeton, N.J.: Princeton University Press, 1959), p. 117ff.

5 David Easton, *The Political System* (New York: Alfred A. Knopf, Inc., 1953), p. 221. See also A. J. Ayer, *Language, Truth and Logic* (London: Victor Gollancz, Ltd., 1936; 2d ed., 1946), especially chap. 6; and C. L. Stevenson, *Ethics and Language* (New Haven, Conn.: Yale University Press, 1944).

6 Easton, *op. cit.,* p. 222. (Italics added.)

7 A. J. Ayer, *Language, Truth and Logic.* Reprinted through permission by Dover Publications, New York 14, N.Y., 1953, p. 107.

"If now I generalize my previous statement and say, 'Stealing money is wrong,' I produce a sentence which has no factual meaning—that is, expresses no proposition which can be either true or false. It is as if I had written 'Stealing money!!'—where the shape and thickness of the exclamation marks show, by a suitable convention, that a special sort of moral disapproval is the feeling which is being expressed."

8 T. D. Weldon, *The Vocabulary of Politics* (Baltimore: Penguin Books, Inc., 1953), coverpiece.

9 Daniel J. Boorstin, *The Genius of American Politics*. Copyright 1953 by the University of Chicago. (Chicago: University of Chicago Press), pp. 184–185. (Phoenix Books ed.)

10 G. C. Field, *Political Theory* (London: Methuer ⁊ Co., Ltd., 1956), p. 87.

11 *Ibid.*, p. 88. (Italics in original.)

12 See, for example, the extensive discussion of hierarchy, polyarchy, and bargaining in Robert A. Dahl and Charles E. Lindblom, *Politics, Economics, and Welfare* (New York: Harper & Brothers, 1953).

13 Field, *op. cit.*, p. 89.

14 Robert A. Dahl, *A Preface to Democratic Theory*. Copyright 1956 by the University of Chicago. (Chicago: University of Chicago Press), p. 132.

15 Ranney and Kendall, *op. cit.*, p. 21. (Italics added.)

16 W. T. Stace, *The Destiny of Western Man* (New York: Reynal & Hitchcock, Inc., 1942), pp. v–vi.

17 Field, *op. cit.*, p. 92.

18 These views, as I have presented them, are obviously highly stylized and as they stand should be attributed to no particular writer. The difference of opinion to which I call attention is, however, very real and can be found in a great variety of literature. See, for example, Arnold Brecht, "Beyond Relativism in Political Theory," a report on a round-table discussion, *American Political Science Review*, vol. 41 (1947), p. 470.

19 Brecht, *Political Theory* . . . , p. 8.

20 *Ibid.*, p. 9. (Italics in original.) See also in the same work Brecht's very interesting discussion of what he calls "professional escapes" from this problem (pp. 10–14).

21 Bertrand Russell, *The Problems of Philosophy* (New York: Oxford University Press, 1959; first published, 1912), p. 7.

22 Morton White, *Religion, Politics and Higher Learning: A Collection of Essays* (Cambridge, Mass.: Harvard University Press, 1959), p. 1.

23 Morton White, *The Age of Analysis* (Boston: Houghton Mifflin Company, 1955).

24 White, *Religion Politics* . . . , pp. 1–2.

25 *Ibid.*

26 *Ibid.*, p. 9. I suggest that White's essay "The Social Role of Philosophy," to which I have referred, is well worth reading in its entirety.

2

CONFUSION, PERPLEXITY, FRUSTRATION: THE PRESENT STATE OF JUSTIFICATION

We are leaping into the middle of what has been one of the most perplexing intellectual problems of modern times. Ignorance of the myriad concerns of other disciplines alone prevents me from saying the *most* perplexing intellectual problem of modern times. In various quarters it is asserted that political philosophy is dead.[1] If this is true, as in one sense I think it is, it is the very problem we must deal with that has killed it. Modern scientific thought has blown such a gaping hole in the edifice of traditional political philosophy that its adherents have turned to historical, textual analysis, "rediscovering some deservedly obscure text or reinterpreting a familiar one,"[2] or to "using low-powered logic on traditional technical problems in an essentially quixotic way."[3]

Indeed, the problem is apparently so formidable that one struggles almost in vain for a place to begin. Much has been written in recent years on the problem of absolutism and relativism in philosophy and politics. The issue here is the connection or lack of connection between certain philosophical systems and certain political systems. Because most of this discussion concerns in one way or another the philosophical support that can be offered for democracy, a look at this debate is perhaps a good way to begin our investigation.[4]

It is significant that we find ourselves beginning by discussing a dichotomy. Anyone who undertakes a generous sampling of the literature on this subject will, it is safe to say, come away with two overriding impressions. One is a general feeling of confusion, perplexity, and frustration. The other is the feeling that one must ultimately choose between two mutually exclusive alternatives. Eventually I shall want to argue that the former is the consequence of the latter and that, by dissolving this apparently inescapable dichotomy, we shall be able to eliminate the confusion, perplexity, and frustration as well. To do this is one of the primary objectives of this essay; but to do it well will require a series of short and careful steps.

Let us begin by examining with some care this absolutism-relativism controversy. Professor William Ebenstein has brought together four essays that reflect varying points of view.[5] The first of these is by the philosopher Bertrand Russell; the second, by political and legal theorist Hans Kelsen; the third, by René de Visme Williamson, who approaches political problems from a Christian point of view; and the fourth, by the British sociologist Morris Ginsberg. As it happens, all these men are in sympathy with democracy, and therefore the possibility of a justification for democracy is one of their central concerns.

We cannot, of course, reproduce these arguments in their entirety here. It will, however, be profitable to examine some of their major points in order to see more clearly the complex nature of the subject with which we are dealing. Russell is mainly concerned with showing the relationship between philosophical absolutism and political absolutism on the one hand, and between philosophical empiricism and democracy on the other. At its core his argument is apparently a historical one. In other words, Russell wants to say that in general philosophical absolutists have argued as well for some kind of political authoritarianism. Plato and Hegel, of course, serve as prime examples. In addition, authoritarian political regimes have often looked to philosophical absolutism for support. Thus, the Communist Party continually invokes Marxian "scientific truth," which is no doubt more accurately described

as a philosophical absolutism. For the Marxist, there is nothing
tentative about the dialectic of history. In the same way the
Nazis looked to Hegelian idealism on those occasions when
they thought justification was desirable. Russell expends most
of his energy attacking absolutism, especially that of Hegel.
This argument, in addition to being rather persuasive, is one
of the most delightful pieces of philosophical polemic to be
found anywhere.[6] Now it may be that in so attacking absolutism Russell is implying that absolutism is no support for anything—something that we shall want to say later. Russell
certainly does say that Hegel's preference for the Prussian
state does not follow *logically* from his absolutism, but just
what the connection *is* is difficult to decide on the basis of Russell's account.

Similarly for Russell, empiricism is connected with democracy; thus, John Locke the great empiricist was also John Locke
the democrat. "The only philosophy that affords a theoretical
justification of democracy in its temper of mind," Russell
argues, "is empiricism." This "theoretical justification" is unfortunately not forthcoming. Russell rightly draws a parallel
with the empiricist's "temper of mind," but he nowhere gives
a reason for adhering to democracy without reservation, which
after all is what a "justification" requires. On the contrary,
Russell's plain implication is that we must be tentative even
about democracy itself. "The genuine Liberal does not say
'this is true'; he says, 'I am inclined to think that under some
circumstances this opinion is probably the best.' *And it is only
in this limited and undogmatic sense that he will advocate
democracy.*"[7] Thus, it is clear that Russell does not give any
reason to support democracy without equivocation. In this
sense he has not solved our problem for us—he has not provided a justification. He is ultimately a relativist; that is, he is
not willing to stand without qualification on democracy,
though he clearly prefers it. I suspect he is unwilling to sub-
scribe unreservedly to democracy because he cannot accept
the metaphysical apparatus he thinks accompanies such a

position. The rigid dichotomy thus operates even on Russell. Unwilling to be an absolutist, he therefore must ultimately be a relativist.

I have alleged that this is a confusing, perplexing, and frustrating subject matter; yet, so far is seems clear enough. If we passionately desire a justification for democracy, we may indeed be frustrated by being told that there is no such thing; but so far we are not particularly confused. Consider, however, this statement from the essay of Kelsen, whose general argument parallels that of Russell: "Tolerance, minority rights, freedom of speech, and freedom of thought, so characteristic of democracy, have no place within a political system based on the belief in absolute values." Now Kelsen gives us some plausible reasons for this contention. "This belief," he says, "irresistibly leads—and always has led—to a situation in which the one who assumed to possess the secret of the absolute good claims to have the right to impose his opinion as well as his will upon the others who are in error."[8] If there is an absolute good, why let an obviously ignorant majority make political decisions? Plato, the philosophical absolutist *par excellence,* faced this problem and developed his philosopher-king to meet it, rejecting majority rule as nonsense. Only by denying absolute values, Kelsen argues, does democracy make sense:[9]

> If, however, it is recognized that only relative values are accessible to human knowledge and human will, then it is justifiable to enforce a social order against reluctant individuals only if this order is in harmony with the greatest possible number of equal individuals, that is to say, with the will of the majority. It may be that the opinion of the minority, and not the opinion of the majority, is correct. Solely because of this possibility, which only philosophical relativism can admit—that what is right today may be wrong tomorrow—the minority must have a chance to express freely their opinion and must have full opportunity of becoming a majority.

Clearly, this argument is not simply nonsense; it contains a measure of truth. But let us ask two questions. Suppose there is a monarch who is quite willing to admit that "what is right today may be wrong tomorrow," is willing to listen to anyone's opinion, but simply retains all power of decision for himself because he wants to. One day a citizen comes to this monarch and says, "You should give up your throne and allow the majority of the people to make decisions." We can imagine the monarch scratching his right ear with his scepter, looking quite pensive, and replying, "That is a very interesting suggestion, but unfortunately it might be wrong." What will our relativist citizen then say to our relativist monarch?

We noted above Kelsen's allegation that tolerance, minority rights, etc., have no place in a system based on absolute values. However, the following question may be asked: "What if tolerance, minority rights, etc., *are* the absolute values?" I trust that now the skeptics among us will begin to see why we contended that this subject matter was confusing, perplexing, and frustrating. René de Visme Williamson makes just the point against Kelsen that our question suggests. "It is high time," he says, "that we straighten out our thinking on this matter and realize that those who were the historic and truly great thinkers and champions of democracy believed in absolute values and took their stand there."[10] Williamson refers to the words "the laws of nature and of nature's God" in the Declaration of Independence and enumerates the absolutes as the rights to equality, life, liberty, the pursuit of happiness, limited government, and revolution. "We are entitled," says Williamson, "to conclude, therefore, that the signers of the American Declaration of Independence were inspired by a philosophy that is completely alien to political relativism. They took a firm stand on absolute values and had the courage to be dogmatic." The argument then, of course, continues that relativism by its very nature can supply no justification, and that not only is absolutism an historically accurate description of the formation of democracy but it is also essential to its preservation.

We well know that Williamson did not invent these words, that they really are there in the Declaration of Independence. We also understand that relativism by definition cannot "jus-

tify" anything; yet we feel the need for justification. Must it
now be said that Kelsen is talking nonsense? I think not, for
surely there *is* something plausible in connecting relativism
with democracy and absolutism with despotism.

Before concluding, we must give our last essayist, the sociologist Ginsberg, his chance to clear away this confusion. Ginsberg shows promise early in the essay when he tells us:[11]

> If democracy is to be justified, we need a surer foundation than
> ethical relativity. This indeed is a truism, since if moral judgments are
> emotive or express the demands of groups, the term justify has no
> meaning other than "persuade or coerce." In rejecting ethical rela-
> tivism we are thus insisting that there is such a thing as a rational
> justification of democratic policy.

So far so good. But what is the justification that Ginsberg proposes? "I think the most promising line of approach is to say
that democracy . . . is considered good because on the whole it
is the best device for securing certain elements of social justice." This begins to sound a little strange already; but when
we hear from Ginsberg that these "elements of social justice"
are "equality" and "freedom," we may fairly wonder how the
above "promising" remarks were ever made. In short, Ginsberg
wants us to "justify" democracy by positing two of its basic
elements as given. Apparently, he conceives of democracy as
equivalent to majority rule, and we must agree that social
science can show on the basis of empirical evidence that the
majority principle is in one sense at least a good, if not the
best, way of maximizing freedom and equality. If this were all
that is involved in justifying democracy, the problem would be
small indeed. Surely, however, this is not the problem which
worries us. The problem of justifying democracy is just as
much a problem of justifying freedom and equality as it is of
justifying majority rule or what might be called a "democratic
institutional arrangement." In addition, of course, social science cannot justify even majority rule in a philosophical sense
but can only show that it seems to work efficiently given
certain goals. For precisely this reason the instrumental dem-

ocratic theorists, whom we discussed earlier, carefully avoid
any notion of philosophical justification. In a fundamental
sense it is fair to say that Ginsberg is actually a relativist, regardless of his protestations. To posit goals is not to justify
them, and to show that somehow they "work" is only to justify them in a relative sense.[12]

In presenting certain points contained in these four
essays, we have to some extent been critical of each of them.
Let me, however, reemphasize that this is not to say that all or
any one of the essays is complete nonsense. In fact, each may
be read with considerable profit. What is most interesting
about these essays is that any one of them read alone is rather
persuasive. When they are read together, however, the situation is quite different. Only the most dogmatic or the most
perceptive reader could fail to be perplexed by the following
conclusions:

We are told that democracy is philosophical relativism in
action *and* that democracy has and requires absolute standards.

We are told that absolute standards lead to totalitarianism
and that totalitarianism is relativism in practice.

We are told that relativism cannot justify anything *and* that
relativism justifies democracy.

We are told that democracy is historically associated with
relativism *and* that democracy is historically associated with
absolutism.

What is puzzling here is that none of these claims is obviously false. On the contrary, each seems to be in some sense accurate. Something is clearly amiss in this literature. What is
required is a very careful unraveling of this extraordinary
ball of twine, and this is surely a task for the analytical political
philosophy discussed earlier.

Underlying this discussion is the notion of a necessary dichotomy between absolutism and relativism. We ourselves
have operated on this assumption in criticizing the essays. Russell and Kelsen proclaim relativism because they cannot accept

the grounds of absolutism. Williamson proclaims absolutism because he cannot accept the consequences of relativism, while Ginsberg tries to avoid the issue by calling for an exhaustive study of the facts. We shall contend that this dichotomy is a false one, imposed by deeply rooted, but nonetheless faulty, habits of thought. When this fundamental mistake has been corrected, these strange and perplexing contradictions which have just been examined will be dispelled, and we shall perhaps understand democracy better than before.

Of course, this will not be easy. We shall have to dig deep—far under our political preferences—and examine what should be meant by the term "proof," by "justification," and ultimately by "democracy" and its aspects, political equality, majority rule, and minority rights.

NOTES

[1] Robert A. Dahl, "Political Theory," *World Politics,* vol. XI (October, 1958), p. 89. See also, Morton White, *Religion, Politics and Higher Learning* (Cambridge, Mass.: Harvard University Press, 1959), p. vii.

[2] Dahl, *loc. cit.*

[3] White, *op. cit.,* p. 3.

[4] There is so much literature bearing on this subject that I am certain I cannot cite it all. In addition to the essays reprinted in William Ebenstein's *Modern Political Thought,* which are to be treated in some detail, and works already cited (Brecht's *Political Theory* and his "Beyond Relativism in Political Theory," Weldon's *The Vocabulary of Politics,* and Stace's *The Destiny of Western Man*), we should mention Leo Strauss, *Natural Right and History.* Copyright 1953 by the University of Chicago. (Chicago: University of Chicago Press); Sidney Hook, "The Philosophical Presuppositions of Democracy," *Ethics,* vol. LII (April, 1942), pp. 275–308; Francis M. Myers, *The Warfare of Democratic Ideals* (Yellow Springs, Ohio: The Antioch Press, 1956); John H. Hallowell, *The Moral Foundation of Democracy.* Copyright 1954 by the University of Chicago. (Chicago: University of Chicago Press); John H. Hallowell, "Politics and Ethics," *American Political Science Review,* vol. XXXVIII (August, 1944), pp. 639–655; J. Roland Pennock, "Reason, Value Theory, and the Theory of Democracy," *American Political Science Review,* vol. XXXVIII

(October, 1944), pp. 855–875; and Gabriel A. Almond, Lewis A. Dexter, W. F. Whyte, and John Hallowell, "Politics and Ethics—A Symposium," *American Political Science Review*, vol. XL (April, 1946), pp. 283–312. Arnold Brecht has also contributed a number of articles bearing on the subject, most of which are reprinted in Morris D. Forkosch (ed.), *The Political Philosophy of Arnold Brecht* (New York: Exposition Press, 1954).

5 William Ebenstein, *Modern Political Thought: The Great Issues*, 2d ed. (New York: Holt, Rinehart and Winston, Inc., 1960).

6 "Of this he [Hegel] gives the following definition: '*The Absolute Idea*. The idea, as unity of the subjective and objective Idea, is the notion of the Idea—a notion whose object is the Idea as such, and for which the objective is Idea—an Object which embraces all characteristics in its unity.' I hate to spoil the luminous clarity of this sentence by any commentary, but in fact, the same thing would be expressed by saying 'The Absolute Idea is pure thought thinking about pure thought.' " Russell in Ebenstein, *op. cit.*, p. 14.

7 *Ibid.*, pp. 17–18. (Italics added.)

8 Kelsen in Ebenstein, *op. cit.*, p. 27.

9 *Ibid.*, p. 28.

10 Williamson in Ebenstein, *op. cit.*, pp. 35–36.

11 Ginsberg in Ebenstein, *op. cit.*, pp. 46–47.

12 See the review article by R. H. Turner, *Ethics*, vol. LXIX (April, 1959), pp. 209–211; and note this comment by J. W. N. Watkins in *Mind*, vol. LXVII (October, 1958), p. 569: "Professor Ginsberg is especially opposed to ethical relativism . . . his intention is to develop a 'rational ethic'; but his antinaturalism [absolutism] makes the actual completion of this task impossible." Ginsberg's argument parallels that of T. D. Weldon, which we shall examine more carefully in a more appropriate context.

3

THE ANATOMY OF THE ABSOLUTISM-RELATIVISM CONTROVERSY

We have spoken of the apparently necessary dichotomy between absolutism and relativism and have tried to see how it affected a philosophical approach to the problem of democracy. I think it is safe to say that we all have a "feeling for" this dichotomy; that is to say, it seems somehow correct. It appears that one must inevitably be either an absolutist or a relativist on matters of ultimate choice or commitment. If we are willing to say flatly that "democracy is the best form of government," we must somehow have absolute, incontrovertible proof or at least believe that such proof exists and can be discovered. On the other hand, if we are willing to say only that "democracy appears to be the best form of government on the basis of this vast heap of empirical evidence" or that "it is best given certain preferred goals," somehow we are still relativists despite our protestations to the contrary.

This dichotomy, as we have suggested, establishes two camps and has two main consequences for a philosophy or a philosophical justification of democracy. One group, feeling the necessity of absolute proof, admits the existence of absolute values and then goes about the business of showing that democracy follows from them. The other group denies the very possibility of absolute proof of the kind advocated by the first group and either becomes avowedly relativistic (Kelsen) or purports to deny relativism and to look for the next best proof, namely, empirical evidence (Ginsberg). Eventually we shall want to examine both the relativist and the absolutist arguments in greater detail; but now, after having seen the differ' ences between these views, it is of the utmost importance to see their similarities or points of agreement.[1]

The history of ideas is generally written in terms of the differences and controversies among varying schools of thought; indeed, this is the kind of thing to which we attend even if we are not writing histories of thought. Accordingly, we have focused on the differences between absolutists and relativists. Significant disagreement, however, generally if not always presupposes some kind of agreement. In simple terms, we may say that people must agree to disagree. But there is much more involved than this statement indicates. "Constructive ideas are generally introduced amidst a maze of polemic. But beneath the polemic the parties of a dispute are almost certainly making common assumptions, focusing attention on the same kinds of question, agreeing that such questions are the important ones; and they are generally failing to be self-critical at common points."[2]

Thus, we have suggested that absolutists and relativists share the opinion that the dichotomy between absolutism and relativism is a necessary one; however, we must go deeper in order to see in what this agreement consists. There is at the core of this dispute an agreement on the nature of proof that is so basic it is never challenged; as a matter of fact, it is never even consciously articulated. Furthermore, it is this agreement about proof, accepted uncritically, that forces the absolutism-relativism dichotomy upon us. By becoming "self-critical" about this common assumption, absolutists and relativists alike will find their positions difficult to maintain, and some other more sensible alternative can be produced.

Let us take a close look at the controversy and in this way concentrate our attention on the nature of proof. What would we take to be absolute proof of the proposition "democracy is the best form of government"? Admittedly, there is something *prima facie* peculiar about this question. Some philosophers would say that the inclusion of the word "best" makes our proposition not a proposition at all and that we are talking nonsense when we ask for absolute proof of it.[3] Let us, however, put this objection aside for the moment. We must, after all, first raise the question in order to see how this objection comes to be invoked against it.

Laying the sophistication of modernity aside, what *would* we take to be absolute proof of such a proposition? Clearly, we would want to establish a general truth and then deduce this particular proposition from it. We would want the proposition "democracy is the best form of government" to be the conclusion of a syllogism with premises that were known to be true. If the major premise is filled by some appropriate general truth, democracy supposedly can be seen to follow as a conclusion. In this way, equality or individual rights are said to follow, for example, from the fact that all men are created in the image of God. We shall have more to say about this later.

Does the arch opponent of absolutism, the relativist, deny that a valid syllogism of this kind would constitute the best proof—in fact, the only absolute proof? Not really. Of course, relativism is a very broad denomination, and hence we generalize with considerable risk. However, we introduce this point in order to advance a philosophical investigation, not to make a statement about the behavior of any and all relativists. Whatever may be the aberrations, clearly the mainstream of relativism grants that deduction is a valid form of inference but in turn objects to absolutist procedure in political philosophy by denying the possibility of proving the major premise in the first place. Two centuries of philosophical investigation are relevant at this point, but there is no time to detail their analyses here. Arguments about the absolute heterogeneity of the "is" and the "ought," the nature of metaphysical statements, and the emotive character of value judgments all may be put to use by the relativist. All we need to grasp here, however, is that the objection is not to deduction per se but to the possibility of using deduction in moral or political philosophy. T. D. Weldon, for example, after having argued that philosophers' attempts to rest political systems on philosophical foundations are pointless, concludes that: "They fail because they mistake the job which philosophical thinking about politics is capable of doing."[4] In other words, they fail because they try to deduce when no deducing is possible.

Having eliminated the possibility of deductive proof, the relativist sees two alternatives. The first is simply to say that no ultimate proof of the proposition is possible and to stop there. This is relativism pure and simple. The second possibility is to treat the proposition "democracy is the best form of government" not as the conclusion of a syllogism but as an empirical hypothesis. The idea here is to establish empirically what people want and to show empirically that democratic institutions are most likely to satisfy these wants. This is relativism with a remedy. The move here is from deductive proof to inductive proof. If deductive proof is impossible, then, it is argued, inductive proof, while not establishing certainty, is the only possible alternative.

Now we must inquire what absolutism has to say about inductive proof. The argument is that inductive proof is not satisfactory, because by its very nature it cannot establish the absolute certainty of any proposition. A counter instance is always possible; thus, inductive proof can only be probable and never absolute. It cannot therefore justify in any ultimate sense. Notice that there is no objection to induction per se, but merely to its inadequacy in the area of ultimate justification.

What we are seeing here is that the absolutist-relativist dualism is a reflection of a more deeply entrenched dualism in the realm of proof. The common assumption is that there are two and only two forms of proof, namely, inductive and deductive. There is nothing startling about this precept, as anyone who as ever read a textbook on logic knows; nor is there anything particularly illegitimate about it. We may say that it is merely part of the definition of proof that it be either inductive, deductive, or a combination of both. But what makes this assumption (or, if you will, "definition") so important for us is the concomitant assumption that *the justification for democracy is a matter of proof.*

Given these two assumptions, three alternative approaches to the problem of justifying democracy are open:

1. Denying the appropriateness of induction, one may try to show absolute proof (justification) by deduction.
2. Denying the possibility of deduction, one may try for proof (justification) by induction.
3. Denying the possibility of deduction and the appropriateness of induction, one may deny the possibility of proof (justification) at all.[5]

In sum, if the justification for democracy is a matter of proof and if there are two kinds of proof, one may accept one or the other or may accept neither. The fourth possibility, to accept both, is not a genuine possibility in this context because induction would be superflous if deduction were accepted. What we are describing in these three alternatives is the anatomy of the absolutism-relativism controversy reviewed earlier. We were aware that something was wrong in this controversy; to continue the medical metaphor—we perceived something of an intellectual trauma. We now have the beginnings of a diagnosis and may be able to suggest the nature of the cure.

The common underlying assumptions that we pointed out cause the words "proof" and "justification" to be equated. This was indicated by placing "justification" after "proof" in posing the three alternatives. I suggest that this is the crux of the problem. We shall have to show that justification is not always the same thing as proof. When we use the word "justification," we sometimes *do* mean proof. For example, if we look at the conclusion "Socrates is mortal" in terms of the immortal syllogism of which it is a part, we can rightly say that the justification for this conclusion is a deductive proof. Similarly, when we say "the sun rises in the east," we shall be correct if we say that the justification here is an inductive proof.

It does not, however, follow from this that all species of

justification are either deductive or inductive. Unfortunately, this other kind of justification cannot be propounded in a few words. We shall have to move slowly and carefully, but we can at this stage pose some rather provocative questions. Are we justified in saying that proof must be inductive or deductive? If we are (surely most of us would unhesitantly make this assertion, and if we did not, our actions would belie our words), what is the nature of the justification? Do we justify the procedure of deduction by deduction? Do we justify it by induction? And what about the inductive procedure; is it justified by induction or perhaps by deduction? There is assuredly something very peculiar about all this, and we should rightly be puzzled about it.

For the present, it is enough to show that justification and proof have been equated and to cast some doubt on this equation. Now we must look carefully at the attempts to justify democracy by deduction and induction, for only by seeing what *cannot* be done can we see what *can* be done.

NOTES

1 Unfortunately, we must, at least for the present, continue to use these terms "absolutist" and relativist," even though we shall be arguing that they are seriously misleading. The dichotomy is apparently so ingrained in our thinking that we have no better words.

2 James Ward Smith, *Theme For Reason* (Princeton, N.J.: Princeton University Press, 1957), p. 1.

3 Again see A. J. Ayer, *Language, Truth and Logic;* and C. L. Stevenson, *Ethics and Language.*

4 T. D. Weldon, *The Vocabulary of Politics* (Baltimore: Penguin Books, Inc., 1953), coverpiece.

5 My presentation of alternatives is paralleled by Sidney Hook, *Political Power and Personal Freedom* (New York: Criterion Press, Inc., 1959), pp. 41–53. Hook breaks down absolutism into theology, metaphysics, and natural law, giving us three examples of our first alternative, and also lists "preference" (relativism) and "hypothesis" (induction). Significantly, these are the only alternatives that "can be offered."

4

THE FUTILITY OF ABSOLUTISM

The preceding discussion has been rather unkind to the absolutists. We have not accepted the relativist position with all its implications, but we have inclined to accept the thrust of the relativist-positivist attack on absolutism. At least by implication we have assented to the notion that deduction from grand theories of the universe or of man makes no sense in political philosophy. This implication does not proceed from misunderstanding; we do want to say explicitly that the deductive-absolutist position is a fallacious one. We must do more than merely *allege,* however; we must *show* carefully and in some detail why this assertion is valid.

In our analysis of the absolutist-relativist controversy, we found it necessary and desirable to break down the argument into a set of simple alternatives. Recall now the statement of the alternative that characterized absolutism: "Denying the appropriateness of induction, one may try to show absolute proof by deduction." On the basis of this description of absolutism, we might expect to find the absolutist argument expressed in rather short essays consisting entirely of a set of syllogisms. We shall, however, look in vain for such a tight, logical presentation. If we do look at the actual literature of absolutism, we find rather substantial volumes written in a style that is anything but syllogistic, works in which the words "deduce" or "deduction" are rarely, if ever, used. Let us be perfectly clear about this. As far as I am aware, no one has ever flatly said that he was *deducing* democracy from some general truth. Nor has anyone ever put his argument for democracy in strict syllogistic form. Because candor is essential in these complex matters, let it be said that we do not want to put our-

selves in the position of having defeated deduction only to have
the absolutist retort with an unsettling "I never said that I *was*
deducing."

An example will perhaps be helpful in understanding what
is at issue here. It is commonplace in writings on democracy to
find statements such as "every man should have one vote and
only one vote" and "all men are created in the image of God."
It is equally commonplace to find the notion that these statements are somehow connected. We are often told that the political maxim "every man should have one vote and only one vote"
rests upon, is supported by, follows from the metaphysical-
religious truth that "all men are created in the image of God."
This line of reasoning is, of course, quite familiar. We would,
however, be sorely tried to cast this inference into a syllogism
that would satisfy the canons of strict deducibility. First of all,
we would have the much-discussed move from an "is" to an
"ought" on our hands, as well as many other difficulties. Thus
it is that writers who want to make this kind of inference do
not profess to deduce in any very rigorous sense but simply allow those vague words "rests upon" or "follows from" to carry
the burden of argument.[1]

But what, we may fairly ask, *is* going on under the smoke
screen set up by "rests upon" or "follows from"? Clearly, one
who uses these words in this way *may* mean a number of different things. I suggest, however, that what is usually going on
under the mist of the absolutist argument is deduction of a
rather loose and uncritical kind. The deductive thought model
is being used either as an ideal or just uncritically. The absolutist is either *trying* to deduce or he may even think that he *is*
deducing. We shall shortly be examining a well-known example of this kind of argument, and this examination will, I
think, corroborate the present point.

I think that we are making sense when we talk about and
attack deduction in this context, even though the absolutists
do not give us complete syllogisms and even though they do
not often say that they *are* deducing. The point, however,

is a difficult one to make. Perhaps another example will
help us to be clear. Suppose that we have before us two putative
syllogisms:

      1. All men are mortal.
         Socrates is a man.
         Therefore, Socrates is mortal.

      2. All men are mortal.
         Fala is a dog.
         Therefore, Fala is mortal.

There is a sense in which we can say that example (1) is deduction whereas (2) is not deduction but merely a string of words.
Although in this sense (2) is not deduction, it is still reasonable
to say that it is an attempt at deduction, that the deductive
thought model is being used. This is very like what we are
saying about the argument that says "every man should have
one vote and only one vote" follows from the fact that all men
are created in the image of God. The intent here is "deductive," whether or not any genuine deduction does in fact
occur.

    There is yet another difficulty we must guard against in this
line of analysis. As Smith remarks, "The reason political
theory is such a difficult subject is that political philosophers
are seldom precise, and when you *make* them precise they can
always say that you have not understood what they meant."[2]
Suppose that the absolutist flatly says that he is not deducing
and then proceeds to turn our own argument against us. He
may say, "I agree with your previous point that it is a mistake
to equate justification with deductive or inductive proof, and
what I am doing here *is* justifying without deducing or inducing." Presumably, our attack on deduction would miss this
man completely. There are two points to be made here. First,
in order to grant this objection to our attack, we would have to
be convinced that deduction, in the sense of the use of the deductive thought model, was not in fact taking place. Secondly,

in order to be moved by this argument, we would have to be convinced that his line of reasoning, whatever he wanted to call it, was satisfactory.[3] And this, we must remember, is the crucial test. Whatever words we may use in our analysis, and whatever words the absolutist may use in presenting his argument, the question remains the same: *Does this argument justify democracy?*

We have, therefore, two arguments to make: (1) Democracy cannot be justified by strict deduction from any grand theory of the universe or of the nature of man. (2) The loose brand of "deduction" or "inference" engaged in by the absolutist thinkers does not justify democracy. The essentials of the first point are fairly straightforward and simple. A genuinely exhaustive account would, however, be quite complex and would require much more time and space than we have a right to spend here. The thousands of pages written on logic testify to this fact. Nonetheless, we can state the conviction and, I think, with some clarity substantiate it. The second point will be somewhat more difficult to establish, but with the help of our analysis of the first point it can be done.

We can begin by asking what kind of conclusion would the would-be deducer of democracy want to come to. I take it that he would want to show an ultimate sanction for, or an absolute demonstration of, a proposal such as "democracy ought to be adopted." The selection of particular words to fill the conclusion in question is less important than seeing what the nature of the conclusion would have to be. I chose the words "democracy ought to be adopted" because this is the best way I can find to express the necessary characteristics. I use "necessary" in the sense of "necessary for the absolutist." For the absolutist, there can be nothing tentative about the conclusion; it must be absolutely obligatory, absolutely "true," absolutely "right," apart from whether or not anyone prefers it. This is true by definition, for to hedge on any one of these points would be to cease being an absolutist. A statement such as "democracy is the best form of government" would work in this context if "best" were taken to imply "ought to be adopted." Lest the semantics of the matter confuse us, "democracy ought to be adopted" seems the best way to express it.

The attempt to prove this conclusion by deduction would, of course, involve a syllogism or a set of syllogisms. We would do well therefore to investigate the nature of syllogisms and/or deductive inference at the outset. Just what is it that allows us to make a deductive inference? A valid deduction is made when it follows that if the premises are true the conclusion must be true also. This statement is, of course, a well-known and generally accepted definition of deduction.[4] It is just what we *mean* by deduction; but we need to look a little further. Let us put that old war horse of deduction on the table before us again:

> All men are mortal.
> Socrates is a man.
> Therefore, Socrates is mortal.

Clearly, this is a case where if the premises are true the conclusion must be true also. What is of crucial importance for us is that this syllogism does not *prove* that the entity of flesh and bone which perambulated the Athenian market place in the fifth century B.C. was mortal. Only the fact that this entity we call Socrates did indeed die "proves" it. We can only be certain that Socrates was mortal by knowing that he died; the syllogism alone cannot do it for us.

By deduction one cannot establish the truth of anything unless he has already in effect decided that it *is* true. Let us amplify this somewhat cryptic statement by pursuing our example. We can begin by observing what happens to the syllogism if we consider the first premise as an empirical proposition. Clearly, we cannot legitimately say that "all men are mortal" if we take the statement as descriptive of the real world. We can only say that all men who have lived and are now dead were mortal, but we cannot be certain about men who are now alive or who are not yet born. Of course, we can be highly confident about a prediction that all present and future living men will die, but we cannot be absolutely sure of it. This is in the nature of an empirical generalization; a counter instance is always possible. What now happens to the conclusion "Socrates is mortal"? It does not follow, for Socrates might be a counter instance.

What we are seeing here is that deductive inference is not an empirical matter. Strictly speaking, it does not inform us about the real world.[5] We can assent to the truth of the conclusion only if two conditions have been met: (1) if we have decided that the premises are true and (2) if the conclusion is implicit in the premises.[6] Thus, in order to establish the conclusion "Socrates is mortal" we must make what is sometimes called "the inductive leap" from "in all cases so far observed men are mortal" to the general statement "all men are mortal." In other words we must *decide* to call the proposition "all men are mortal" true, for if we did not, the conclusion would not follow as was shown above. More than this, it must be that "Socrates is mortal" is implicit in "all men are mortal." To put it more exactly, it must be that what we *mean* by "men" is that Socrates is one of them. We reassert this meaning in the minor premise "Socrates is a man."[7] In order, therefore, to establish a valid deductive inference, we must *decide* to assent to certain truths and must *decide* to use words in a certain way.

It must be emphasized that we are not saying that deductive inference is not of very great value. Natural science could not have made its present progress without that purely deductive system of inference called mathematics.[8] It is a great convenience to be able to say $1 + 1 = 2$, even though it does not always hold true in the real world (e.g., two equal quantities of mercury when combined equal something slightly less than two). The value of deductive inference is heuristic, but in most cases it would be misleading to say *merely* heuristic. Nevertheless, to see, as we have, that it *is* heuristic is to see a limitation, which, while not important in many instances,[9] is of great importance for the would-be deducer of democracy. Before seeing just why this is so, we must look more carefully at what would be involved in deducing an imperative such as "democracy ought to be adopted."

If it is true, as we have tried to show, that the conclusion of a deductive inference must be implicit in the premises, it must also be that an imperative conclusion is contained in its premises. As philosopher R. M. Hare puts it, "It follows that, if there is an imperative in the conclusion, not only must *some* imperative appear in the premises, but that very imperative must be itself implicit in them."[10] For example, the imperative "do not tell this lie" could not be deduced from premises such as "every lie is an untruth" and "this is a lie." The inference, if it is to be an inference, must proceed something like this:

> Never lie.
> This is a lie.
> Therefore, do not tell this lie.

It is easy to see that this syllogism satisfies the standards stated above but that a syllogism composed of purely indicative premises would not.[11] The very imperative expressed in the conclusion is implicit in the first premise; and if it were not, the inference could not be said to be valid.[12]

Thus it happens that, when we deduce a particular imperative from a more general one, we are not deciding something *new* but are only being consistent with something we have already decided. If, as we have shown, one cannot arrive at an imperative *by deduction* from purely indicative premises, then the whole notion of reaching any kind of obligatory, imperative conclusions by *deducing* from first premises of an indicative kind is erroneous. It is, therefore, small wonder that the absolutists shy away from any notion of strict deducibility.

On the basis of this examination of what strict deducibility *would* be like in the context of political philosophy, we are able to get certain valuable insights into what absolutist political philosophy is *really* like. Let us reiterate certain points gleaned from our analysis above, and let us hold them firmly in mind as we examine a typical absolutist "justification" of democracy.

1. There is no logical progression from purely indicative premises to imperative conclusions.
2. Any deductively valid conclusion, including an imperative one, must be implicit in the premises.
3. It is necessary to *decide* that the premises are valid if the conclusion is to be valid.

It must surely be clear that this set of rules makes it impossible for anyone to promulgate by strict deduction a justification for democracy which purports to be absolutely binding because it is based on the way the world really is. It is equally clear that one *can* cast his own preference for democracy in deductive form; that is, the argument could consist in the deductive exfoliation of an imperative premise that was simply held to be valid. This, it seems to me, is the procedure followed by absolutist political philosophers, whether they are supporting democracy or some form of authoritarianism.

Absolutist political philosophy, whether it be Hegelian, Marxist, or Thomistic, on its surface appears to be composed of a broad, general *Weltanschauung* and a number of political proposals alleged to "follow from" or "be entailed by" the *Weltanschauung*. It is our task to discover just how these *Weltanschauungen* are actually related to the political proposals they presumably support. We are, of course, specifically interested in the particular kind of metaphysical theory that is typically used as a support for democracy. There is perhaps no other way of understanding the nature of these proposals than by carefully examining a particular example. This we shall presently do; but to set our line of approach it is necessary to make some very general introductory remarks on the peculiar character of this thing called *Weltanschauung*.

Following Professor Smith's analysis, there are three general observations to be made. "First: one of the primary characteristics of any *Weltanschauung* worth considering is its capacity

to provide a linguistic recipe for describing *any* fact with which
it is confronted. . . . In one sense, the whole point of a metaphysical theory is that it provides, if it is successful, a set of
terms general enough to enable one to discuss anything whatsoever."[13] A particular metaphysical theory, although it may
serve many additional purposes, at least provides an all-encompassing phraseology. To say that a *Weltanschauung* is all-
encompassing is, of course, a tautology. We may also say that
(this again is in a sense obvious) a metaphysical theory is profoundly nonempirical. These two observations are two sides
of the same coin. Perhaps we should do well to emphasize this
point by way of example.

The notion of an all-encompassing teleology is a view of the
world quite familiar to everyone. We may posit this view in
simple form by the statement "everything which exists has a
purpose." Sir Isaiah Berlin makes our point quite clearly
with regard to this particular *Weltanschauung*.[14]

> This attitude is profoundly anti-empirical. We attribute purpose
> to all things and persons not because we have evidence for this hy-
> pothesis; for if there were a question of evidence for it, there could
> in principle be evidence against it; and then some things and events
> might turn out to have no purpose, and therefore, in the sense used
> above, be incapable of being explained at all; but this cannot be, and
> is rejected in advance, *a priori*. We are plainly dealing not with an
> empirical theory but with a metaphysical attitude which takes for
> granted that to explain a thing, to describe it as it "truly" is, even to
> define it more than verbally, that is, superficially, is to discover its
> purpose. Everything is in principle explainable, for everything has
> a purpose, although our minds may be too feeble or too distraught to
> discover in any given case what this purpose is. On such a view to say
> of things or persons that they exist or are real, yet literally lack a pur-
> pose, whether imposed from the outside or "inherent" or "innate," is
> to say something not false, but literally self-contradictory and there-
> fore meaningless. *Teleology is not a theory, or a hypothesis, but a
> category or a framework in terms of which everything is, or should be
> conceived and described.*

It is easy to see that arguments which attribute everything to
the means of production or to the will of God are of a com-

parable character. Any event can be "explained" in these terms, and the "explanation" cannot be assailed by empirical evidence, for one can always silence a dissenter by saying, "God—or the means of production (depending on where you stand)—works in mysterious ways." So much for the first point, which emphasizes the extreme generality of metaphysical theories.

Explanation of the second point may be facilitated by posing a question. If we are presented with two rival metaphysical views of the world, each of which is undoubtedly internally consistent, how are we to choose between them? As Smith remarks, "Strict rules of logical entailment will govern much of what we do in working out the details of any *Weltanschauung*, but will be powerless as a leverage for recommending the *Weltanschauung*."[15] Here we hark to our earlier remarks on the analytic character of deductive inference. It is entirely possible to *decide* that certain general propositions are true and to develop an entire system from them by deduction, but this says nothing about the validity of the first premises. We may be able to develop valuable proposals for the real world by this method, or we may not. The test is surely "beyond deduction."

The third and final point is the most important and at the same time the most difficult to come to grips with. The rule that "any deductively valid conclusion, including an imperative one, must be implicit in the premises" provides the clue. According to Smith, "The problem of recommending any *Weltanschauung* as a whole and the problem of recommending any specific proposal (either descriptive or otherwise) with which one seeks to associate that *Weltanschauung* are not two different problems such that one passes from one to the other either deductively or inductively. To recommend a general conception of the world *is* to recommend making one's proposals in one way rather than another; but it simultaneously *is* to recommend just those proposals (descriptive or otherwise) rather than others."[16] In other words, one cannot legitimately proceed from the very general premises of a *Weltanschauung,* which in the nature of the case are capable of verbally "explaining" or "justifying" anything, to specific political recommendations unless the political proposals are themselves implicit in the premises of the *Weltanschauung.*

The preceding remarks should be taken as introductory, as setting the tone for what follows. In order to substantiate our point, that metaphysical justifications for democracy are fallacious, we shall, as indicated above, resort to an example. Clearly, any set of proposals that is to be acceptable as justification for democracy must support democracy and democracy alone. It simply would not do to advance proposals that might be used to "justify" democracy at one time and some form of authoritarianism at another. Surely it is clear that an argument for democracy based on proposals of this character cannot be a genuine justification, but only a very elaborate way of stating one's preferences. A true justification must emanate from a valid line of reasoning rooted in something other than preference, reasoning that leads to democracy and excludes any other political system. We cannot demand that it lead us to an absolute obligation to choose one from a number of institutional implementations such as the town meeting, a parliamentary system, a presidential system, bicameralism, or judicial review. But we must demand that a justification, if it is to be acceptable, allow us to uphold without qualification broad principles such as majority rule, protection of minority political rights, and political equality. Anything less than this is either relativistic or wholly beside the point.

I propose that we examine the arguments of two philosophical absolutists who allegedly rest their political proposals on the same set of metaphysical premises but whose proposals nonetheless differ sharply. One thinker argues for an elaborate form of authoritarianism, the other for democracy. The two writers in question are Plato, as represented in the *Republic,* and the American political theorist John H. Hallowell, as represented in his book *The Moral Foundation of Democracy* [17]

This choice seems to me a felicitous one for at least three reasons. First of all, Plato's teachings are well known enough to allow us to refer to them without elaborate explanation. Second, that Hallowell shares the essentials of Plato's metaphysic is made clear in Hallowell's own exposition. Finally, Hallowell is one of the foremost exponents of the modern absolutist argument for democracy and is, therefore, precisely the sort of theorist we are interested in.

What then is the nature of the *Weltanschauung* that is common to both? Here, of course, a certain amount of simplification is a necessity, but conveniently Hallowell does it for us. "My argument," says Hallowell, "will rest upon [note this language] what might be called the principles of classical realism, principles which commend themselves to common sense."[18] Hallowell then proceeds to present a summary of classical realism in terms of three principles. These principles we may fairly take to represent the common metaphysic of Hallowell and Plato, although there are perhaps elements in Hallowell's presentation that are, strictly speaking, more ethical and epistemological than metaphysical. The principles are as follows:[19]

> 1. There exists a meaningful reality whose existence does not depend on our knowledge of it. . . . The world in which we live is an orderly universe—a cosmos, not a chaos.
> 2. . . . man is endowed with a faculty which enables him at least dimly, to grasp the meaning of this reality. . . . Knowledge does not involve the making or constructing of anything, but rather the discovery of what already exists.
> 3. . . . being and goodness belong together. Through knowledge of what we are, we obtain knowledge of what we ought to do. To know what man is, is to know what he should be and do.

Admittedly, it is rather difficult to see what all this has to do with politics. Of course, for our absolutists it is extremely pertinent, and if we examine them in their respective historical circumstances, we can perhaps see why they think so.

Plato has seen his native land defeated in a long and costly war by a unified and tightly disciplined adversary. In his own *polis* he has seen decay under the rule of a shifting, vacillating, sometimes passionate and sometimes indifferent majority. His own wise and distinguished teacher has been convicted of treason by a disorderly mob. Plato finds the situation deplorable and consequently undertakes the construction of a formula for a remedy. If there exists a meaningful reality, he reasons, and if this reality is the criterion of goodness, the remedy must lie in discovering this reality and adhering to it. If the rulers of the state understood this reality, the right decisions could be made, and the chaos and turmoil would be eliminated. What we must do therefore is to devise a system whereby the most capable can be chosen and trained for the all-important job of ruling. We may have to invent some stories in order to convince the many that the capable few should rule, but this does not matter if justice and the good state are the end products. The details of this argument are too familiar to require further discussion here. What we can see from this brief account is that it is wholly possible to make a case for rule by the very few in the language of "classical realism."

Hallowell, on the other hand, lives in what is perhaps the most successful nation in the history of the world, a country that has lived by the principles of political equality, majority rule, and minority rights for over 150 years. But Hallowell sees the system challenged from abroad by systems characterized by arbitrary, one-man rule. These totalitarian systems are, from his point of view, the consequence of denying the existence of an absolute standard of value. Some people (Kelsen, for example) think that such systems are the consequence of *proclaiming* an absolute standard, but Hallowell is apparently untouched by this notion. There is a need, for Hallowell, to reassert the validity of democracy in terms of absolute standards, and he explicitly states his argument in the language of "classical realism." A reality exists and that reality is good. All men are capable of recognizing this reality, and therefore all men are equal. "It is in the light of this law that all men are equal—equal not in wealth, in talents, in physical strength or learning but equal in the capacity to distinguish justice from injustice, right from wrong." This reality which is good and is known to men is natural law, and "it is these two doctrines— the doctrine of natural law and the equality of men—which lie at the foundation of what today we call 'democracy.' . . . "[20]

What we have seen, in this admittedly simplified presentation, are two radically different political proposals stated in the language of the same *Weltanschauung*. And both these proposals are alleged to be supported by or to follow from the *Weltanschauung*. Something is clearly amiss here, but just what is it? Someone might argue that one of the writers is using the *Weltanschauung* correctly, while the other is wrong. One is deducing the proper conclusion, and the other is using an incorrect line of reasoning. But in terms of the rules of deduction discussed above, it is simply absurd to think that either political proposal can be "deduced" from the *Weltanschauung* as it stands. The three premises simply do not "entail," in the sense of "logically deducible from," either democracy or Plato's brand of authoritarianism. In order for deduction to make any sense in this context, it would be necessary to add at least one more premise (a different one, of course, for each argument).[21]

The problem here is that the conclusions, that is, the political proposals, are not implicit in the premises as they stand —and they must be if deduction is to take place. Let us therefore supply the additional premises and see what happens. If for Plato's argument we add the premise "this reality which is good can only be known by a capable and highly trained few," the notion of deduction begins to make more sense. The same holds true for Hallowell if we add a different premise, namely, "this reality which is good can be known by all men." The difference between these two premises is the key to the difference between Plato's authoritarian proposal and Hallowell's democratic one. This is again made clear by Hallowell's own exposition. He is willing to accept Plato's reasoning up to the point where Plato restricts the possibility of knowledge to the few. Consider, for example, this passage:[22]

> Plato believed that in the ideal state political power and love of the good would be combined in the same individuals. This is the essential meaning of his declaration that in the ideal state philosophers will be kings, and kings philosophers. He meant by "philosophers" lovers of wisdom, seekers after the good. Whereas *Plato, however, believed that only a few members of society could ever aspire to a life of virtue* [and remember that for Plato "virtue is knowledge"], *it is the faith underlying modern democracy that all men may aspire to that life of virtue which Plato would restrict to the few.*

Hallowell is willing to follow Plato in the "principles of classical realism," but he must depart from Plato when Plato restricts the possibility of virtue, or knowledge, to the few. Hallowell sees that he cannot make a case for democracy unless all men can acquire this knowledge. *But—and this is the crucial question—who is right, Plato or Hallowell?* My contention is that it is impossible to answer this question by reference to Plato or Hallowell or by use of their method, that is, deduction.

We have said that by adding a fourth premise to the three premises of classical realism the notion of deduction begins to make sense; and this is indeed correct. But why does it make sense? There can be only one reason for this in terms of the rules of deduction—the premise must implicitly state the conclusion.[23] If this is so, however, there is no reason in terms of the principles of classical realism why we should accept either conclusion. Hallowell asks us to accept democracy, and if we ask him why, he can rely upon one of two things. He can point to the three major principles of classical realism on which his argument allegedly rests. Clearly, this will not suffice, for as we saw above no political proposal is logically entailed by these principles. He can, and does in his exposition, point to the three principles of classical realism supplemented by at least the additional premise indicated above. The addition of this premise, however, will not be satisfactory either, because in the nature of the case it has a proposal of democracy implicit in it.

What I am arguing here is that the premise "this reality which is good can be known to all men" is simply another way of saying "all men are equal and should therefore be treated as political equals." Indeed, this must be so if deduction is to make any sense in this context. This fourth premise, which is crucial to Hallowell's argument, is not an independent premise from which democracy somehow "follows"; rather, it is a proposal of democracy couched in the language of classical realism. As Smith explains it, the absolutist "is tricked into supposing that his recommendation 'follows from' his elaborate metaphysic because of the relatively unimportant fact that his metaphysic provides a terminology in which his proposal can be stated."[24]

The issue between Plato and Hallowell is not, therefore, a matter of deduction at all.[25] It is instead a question of deciding to look at politics and the world in general in one way rather than another. Absolutists in political philosophy are really in an impossible position. They profess to present us with a *Weltanschauung* from which a particular political system follows; however, if they leave the *Weltanschauung* in general terms, anything or nothing can follow from it. If, on the other hand, they make their premises specific enough so that a particular political system can be deduced, the premise (or premises) constitutes an implicit proposal of just that political system and therefore cannot furnish good reason for accepting the political system. The fact that one can state a preference for democracy in the language of a particular metaphysic does not give us any reason to accept it as a political system. Students of political thought have long been struck by the fact that democracy has at one time or another derived "support" from a great and diverse variety of metaphysical theories—" . . . in 1890 by the whole apparatus of Calvinist Puritanism; in 1750 to 1800 by a mixture of Lockeism, excessive Newtonianism, French Encyclopedism, and the shallow metaphysics of deism; in 1840 by the wild transcendental orgies of Emerson; in the late nineteenth century by the cosmic evolutionists, by Hegelian idealists, and by the early metaphysical pragmatists; to name only a few highlights."[26] If our analysis is accurate, this diverse list creates no great mystery, for it merely testifies to the fact that political proposals can be presented in metaphysical language. In so far as these arguments pretend to deduce, they are as unconvincing as the argument from classical realism.

Our whole approach to the problem of absolutism as a justification for democracy has, up to this point, been negative. We have tried to show that the entire enterprise is misconceived and that the deductive thought model is inappropriate in this area of investigation. This attack on absolutism is not, however, without its positive aspect. We noted earlier that the only absolute *proof* of democracy or anything else was deductive proof. Now, if it is the case that the only absolute proof is deductive proof *and* that deductive proof is impossible in political philosophy, surely it is nonsense to demand absolute proof in the deductive sense from anyone who proposes a justification of democracy. This is part of what we meant when we said that justification is not always a matter of proof. To comprehend this point is, as I shall try to show, a contribution to political philosophy of considerable value.

NOTES

1 "Who says that political proposals *can,* in any strict sense, be 'deduced' from general theories? The problem may be briefly stated in the following way: A great deal of what passes as political theory is written in a tone which suggests the notion of strict logical deducibility. Political theory bristles with such idioms as 'since (followed by some highly general metaphysical comment), therefore we must . . . ,' or 'unless (some large theory be true), there is no basis for doing so and so,' or 'if (again followed by an enormous idea), then we cannot avoid or we have no choice but. . . . ' " James Ward Smith, *Theme for Reason* (Princeton, N.J.: Princeton University Press, 1957), p. 30.

2 *Ibid.*, p. 33. (Italics in original.)

3 "It is true that if we use the word 'deduce' strictly, it is an egregious mistake to suppose that recommendations to act in certain ways can be deduced from general theories. It is also true that when Hegelians, Marxists, and Thomists [absolutists] speak of their particular political and social proposals as 'entailed by' or 'following from' their large and pretentious metaphysical doctrines they are guilty of irresponsible hocus-pocus." *Ibid.*, p. 35.

4 Cf. Richard Bevan Braithwaite, *Scientific Explanation* (New York: Cambridge University Press, 1953), p. 257.

5 This point is well established by modern philosophy. For example, R. M. Hare tells us, "Few people now think, as Descartes seems to have done, that we can arrive at scientific conclusions about matters of empirical fact, like the circulation of the blood, by deductive reasoning from self-evident first principles. The work of Wittgenstein and others has to a great extent made clear the reasons for the impossibility of doing this." R. M. Hare, *The Language of Morals* (New York: Oxford University Press, 1952), p. 32.

6 The exception to the second condition need not trouble us at present. "We have, therefore, to say that there must be nothing said in the conclusion which is not said implicitly or explicitly in the premises, *except what can be added solely on the strength of definitions of terms.*" *Ibid.*, p. 33. (Italics in original.)

7 " . . . all deductive inference is analytic in character; that is to say, that the function of a deductive inference is not to get from the premises 'something further' not implicit in them (even if that is what Aristotle meant), but to make explicit what was implicit in the conjunction of the premises. This has been shown to follow from the very nature of language; for to say anything we have . . . to obey some rules, and these rules . . . mean, firstly, that to say what is in the premises of a valid inference is to say, at least, what is in the conclusion, and, secondly, that if anything is said in the conclusion which is not said, implicitly or explicitly, in the premises, the inference is invalid." *Ibid.*, pp. 32–33.

8 Likewise, our argument against deduction in political philosophy has nothing to do with deduction used for avowedly heuristic purposes, e.g., as described by Karl Popper in *The Logic of Scientific Discovery* (New York: Basic Books, Inc., 1959). We do not therefore attack the deduction of Anthony Downs, *An Economic Theory of Democracy* (New York: Harper & Brothers, 1957), or Morton Kaplan, *System and Process in International Politics* (New York: John Wiley & Sons, Inc., 1957).

9 It is not very important in our present example, for we do not really expect to find a man who is not mortal. "All men are mortal" while not logically necessary (unless one wants to say that "mortal" is part of the definition of "man") is something almost empirically necessary like "nothing can be faster than the speed of light." Separating the logically and empirically necessary is often a very difficult business; see Norwood Russell Hanson, "Imagining the Impossible," *Analysis*, vol. XIX (March, 1959), pp. 86–92. Perhaps it is fair to say

that the closer a proposition is to empirical necessity, the higher the heuristic
value of an inference drawn from it.

[10] Hare, *op. cit.*, p. 31. (Italics in original.)

[11] There is serious question as to whether or not any kind of deductive
model is helpful in accounting for moral reasoning as it actually occurs. Cf.
Smith, *op. cit.*, pp. 43–45, 86–88; and Mrs. P. R. Foot, "When Is a Principle
a Moral Principle?" *Aristotelian Society Supplementary Volume* XXVIII
(London: Harrison & Sons, Ltd., 1954), pp. 95–110.

[12] This discussion is, of course, a way of detailing or giving reasons for the
oft-made claim that there is no logical bridge between an "is" and an "ought"
or between an indicative and an imperative. It is helpful to see the reasons
rather than simply adhere to the claim as dogma.

[13] Smith, *op. cit.*, p. 37. (Italics in original.)

[14] Isaiah Berlin, *Historical Inevitability* (New York: Oxford University Press,
1954), pp. 14–15. (Italics added.)

[15] Smith, *op. cit.*, p. 37.

[16] *Ibid.*, p. 38. (Italics in original.)

[17] John H. Hallowell, *The Moral Foundation of Democracy.* Copyright 1954
by the University of Chicago. (Chicago: University of Chicago Press). This line
of analysis is suggested to me by Smith's similar comparison of Fichte and
Emerson. Smith, *op. cit.*, pp. 39–49.

[18] Hallowell, *op. cit.*, p. 24. Classical realism is, of course, the name traditionally applied to Platonic doctrines. As Popper explains, "The name
'realism' derives from the assertion that universal objects, for instance, white-
ness, 'really' exist, over and above single things or sets or groups of single
things." Karl R. Popper, *The Poverty of Historicism* (Boston: The Beacon
Press, 1957), p. 28.

[19] Hallowell, *op. cit.*, pp. 24–25.

[20] *Ibid.*, p. 115.

[21] Cf. Smith, *op. cit.*, p. 43.

[22] Hallowell, *op. cit.*, pp. 113–114. (Italics added.)

[23] Clearly, the two additional premises as stated above are not sufficiently
detailed to allow genuine deduction of detailed political proposals, but this
does not impede making the essential points about them.

[24] Cf. Smith, *op. cit.*, pp. 44, 46.

[25] Cf. *ibid.*, p. 48.

[26] *Ibid.*, p 34.

5

RELATIVISM IN DISGUISE

In one sense the arguments we have advanced as a critique of the deductive method in political philosophy are not unprecedented. It is easy enough to find a similar line taken by a number of modern commentators, among them John Dewey, Karl Popper, and T. D. Weldon. Consider, for example, what Weldon has to say about the "foundations" of democracy:[1]

> The metaphysical foundations of democracy then are roughly these: (1) human beings as such ought to be respected because they are endowed with Reason; (2) they are bound only by laws of their own making, and to be bound by such laws is to be free; (3) Reason provides them with a test by which they can satisfy themselves of the appropriateness or otherwise of proposed or actual laws; (4) the test is whether these laws would be acceptable to a community of completely rational beings. I do not suggest that democratic writers and thinkers have all been as metaphysical as that, but I believe that their proofs will not work unless these or very similar premises are accepted.

Weldon is setting up, as we did, metaphysical premises that the would-be deducer of democracy must use if his "proofs" are to "work."

"What we really want to know," Weldon continues, "is what is the use of all this. Suppose we could accept the premises and reasonings, should we be any better off? I think that we should not." Weldon here agrees with us that metaphysical premises do not provide a genuine foundation for democracy:[2]

> The objection to this sort of argument is not merely that it depends for its force on . . . fallacious assumptions . . . but that the conclusions to which it leads are either vacuous or highly disputable and not at all self-evident. . . . It is natural to suppose therefore that we have here fundamental rules from which others can be deduced. If this were so "foundations" would be a suitable word for describing them. But it is not so. Nothing follows from these high abstractions, or if you like anything does. They are not concerned with actual people

but with "real" ["real," of course, in the sense of "classical realism"] or metaphysical ones. By themselves they tell us nothing whatever about how to deal with prisoners of war, criminals, or taxi-drivers. We can derive no actual law by means of them. That is what I mean by saying that as foundations they are useless. They do not and cannot do what they purport to do, that is, serve as axioms from which practical conclusions can be derived.

Weldon attacks, and rightly so, the notion of foundations for political preferences that are conceived as axioms from which the political preferences follow. But—and this, then, is the important question—does it follow from this that the very notion of presenting foundations for political choices (or as we have put it, "justifying" political choices) is erroneous? Weldon certainly thinks so. We quoted him in the introductory section of this essay as saying, " . . . no such foundations exist and . . . all attempts to demonstrate the superiority of the foundations on which democracy rests to those of communism and totalitarianism are pointless." As we said in the introductory chapter, Weldon is right in maintaining that the kind of foundations he is talking about "do not exist" and that it is "pointless" to look for them; *but it does not therefore follow that there are no foundations at all.*

How does Weldon come to this particular conclusion? If justification, or in Weldon's language "the search for foundations," is conceived as a matter of proof and if deductive inference is the only absolute proof, then it does follow that the impossibility of deduction means also the impossibility of justification and/or of establishing foundations. We saw this earlier in our introductory analysis of the absolutism-relativism controversy. It is this identification, this merging, of the notions of proof and justification that leads Weldon astray. "Essentially the search for foundations is a search for proofs . . . ,"[3] according to Weldon's own explicit statement, and the whole tone of his exposition testifies to the correctness of our interpretation.

Given Weldon's rejection of a deductive proof for democracy, we may on the basis of our previous analysis expect him to take one of two approaches to the problem of justifying democracy. As stated earlier, these alternatives were:

a. Denying the possibility of deduction, one may try for proof (justification) by induction.

b. Denying the possibility of deduction and the appropriateness of induction, one may deny the possibility of proof (justification) at all.

These alternatives are in a sense alternatives for the unsophisticated, and Weldon is not so naïve as to fall headlong into the trap set by merging the notions of justification and proof. Weldon senses the existence of a pitfall but, I think, does not quite see where it is. Because he does not walk blindly into one alternative or the other, it is rather difficult to say with precision just where he does come to rest.

If we were to accept Professor Smith's interpretation of Weldon, there would be no difficulty. Smith sees Weldon as simply swallowing our first alternative whole.[4]

> Where does Weldon take us? His argument is that since political proposals cannot be justified as logical entailments of large and moving philosophical theories, they can be justified, if at all, as confirmable empirical hypotheses.

In support of his interpretation, Smith then quotes Weldon:[5]

> . . . when verbal confusions are tidied up most of the questions of traditional political philosophy are not unanswerable. *All of them* are confused formulations of purely empirical difficulties. This does not mean that these are themselves easy to deal with, but it does mean that writers on political institutions and statesmen, not philosophers, are the proper people to deal with them. As empirical questions they do have answers, but the answers are neither simple nor demonstrably and incorrigibly true, nor can they be discovered by any process of non-empirical intuition.

Smith italicizes Weldon's three little words "all of them" and reads far too much into them. Weldon plainly does not say that *all* political proposals must be read as empirical hypotheses to be tested by induction, even though this passage may make it sound that way. Smith has a valid point to make, namely, that all too often the case for empiricism and experimentalism in political studies consists merely in the heaping of scorn upon deductive absolutism;[6] but Weldon does not serve as an altogether good example.[7]

But what conclusions does Weldon come to? Surely Weldon does heap scorn upon deductive absolutism: " . . . the theoretical foundations of political thinking which are claimed by Democracy, Hegelian Idealism, and Marxism are all equally worthless. They do not support the superstructures which they are supposed to support and could not conceivably do so." He contends, however, that to state this is not to give up the game to relativism. " . . . this conclusion is in no way devastating or even alarming. It does not involve cynicism, scepticism, or even the rejection of moral or political evaluations. All that is discarded is some metaphysical lumber."[8] "I do not believe," Weldon declares later on, "that by discarding political foundations or ideologies I am logically committed to political scepticism."[9]

Very well, but where do we go from here? In the first place, a good many political proposals can be considered as empirical hypotheses, the proper test being whether they in fact contribute to a desirable end. " . . . if the National Health Service is considered as a health-promoting institution, its success or failure is demonstrable by reference to infant mortality rates, decreases in the incidence of infectious diseases and so on." Still, contrary to Smith's implication, Weldon judges that from a philosophical point of view this kind of political proposal is not very important. " . . . it still makes sense," says Weldon concerning the National Health Service, "to admit that from this point of view it is successful but to condemn it as a political institution."[10] The important questions are matters of judging the "goodness" or "badness" of political institutions not in so far as they are instrumental to some external goal but in themselves. This kind of ultimate judgment may be called, as Charles S. Hyneman suggests, an "aesthetic" judgment.[11] As a matter

of fact, Weldon rather likes the artistic metaphor and vigor-
ously pursues an artistic analogy.

Relating a particular political proposal to a specified end
does not solve the philosophical problem, as Weldon rightly
perceives. "Yet, if I say 'I know that the National Health Service
reduces infant mortality but I deny that it conduces to the general good,' my statement is quite intelligible, but demands for
statistical evidence in support of it seem to be inappropriate."
The language of means to ends simply does not work for the
important questions of political philosophy according to Weldon. It is not at all helpful to say that a certain political institution is good because it contributes to the general good, for "we
are mistaken in supposing that 'the general good' stands for an
end which can be achieved, like healing sickness or scoring
goals." We can see how properly to assess political proposals "by
considering how we talk about a type of activity different from
that of making and appraising political institutions in which
also the analysis into means and ends breaks down, namely, the
activity of the artist and that of the art critic."[12] Weldon wants
to point out that the artist does not paint pictures with the idea
of making them conform to some specified form and that it
makes sense for an art critic to judge the merits of a painting
even though he has no clear-cut standard as to what constitutes
a "good" painting. It does not for Weldon make sense to talk
about art in terms of means to ends, but it does make sense to
talk about art. In somewhat the same way, political institutions
and statesmen need critics who can judge their merits and de-
merits without reference to an ideal end or form. Weldon
imagines that experienced students of political institutions are
in a position to do this. "Now just as there are experts whose
professions it is to pass judgement on pictures and symphonies,
so there are specialists in political institutions." It is for this
reason "that writers on political institutions and statesmen, not
philosophers, are the proper people to deal with [political prob-
lems]."[13] Weldon does not mean, as Smith apparently thinks,
that political problems should all be treated as empirical

hypotheses subject to confirmation or confutation by reference to statistical evidence. What he does mean is that *experience* in political affairs is relevant, just as experience in artistic affairs is relevant for the art critic. "In fact the crucial question which needs to be answered . . . is not 'What are the best institutions for human beings to live under?' but 'Do we know enough about the facts to be qualified to give helpful advice in this case?,' and it should be remembered that the relevant facts include the traditions, history, geographical conditions, education, and customary standard of living of the people concerned."[14]

Thus, Weldon is saying that, when political judgments are to be made, political scientists and not philosophers are the proper people to ask. This is apparently because political scientists will refer to their experience with and knowledge of politics, which for Weldon is the proper method of evaluation. Philosophers, on the other hand, will try to set up an absolute standard to which the political proposals can be referred—for Weldon, plainly the wrong way of going about it. Nevertheless, political philosophy is not totally useless, according to Weldon. Among other functions, it can work to clarify the language of political science, for "it would be uneconomical to require those whose job it is to investigate, describe, and appraise political institutions to exercise perpetual vigilance over their own linguistic usages." More than this "it is important, too, to work through the competing ideologies and to see them in their proper perspective. Until this is done, they tend to confuse and distort political thinking and to make us forget that governing at any level is essentially a matter of judgement and decision by statesmen and rulers and not a matter of theoretical reasoning."[15] *But the one thing that political philosophy cannot do is what it has always been intended to do, namely, set up standards for the evaluation of political institutions.*

Are we therefore to give up the business of evaluating political institutions? Some such conclusion would seem to follow from the position that Weldon takes, but he is understandably unhappy about this prospect and does his best to fill the gap.

His solution is in a sense straightforward and simple: the evaluation of political institutions is not a philosophical but an empirical problem.[16] Upon careful examination, however, we find it to be neither very simple nor, what is more important, very satisfactory. To say, for example, that X is a better political institution than Y without accepting some kind of standard for evaluation would be utterly meaningless. One simply does not make evaluations without explicitly or implicitly accepting a standard. Although Weldon recognizes this necessity, he is very nervous about this problem of setting up standards, because philosophers have traditionally supported their claims in this area by one or another kind of metaphysical hocus-pocus.

We must therefore *have* standards, but they cannot be philosophical standards. They are, according to Weldon, to be standards based on experience with politics; and for this reason statesmen and political scientists, not philosophers, are the proper people to set them up. But, we must ask ourselves if this delegation of authority makes sense. No one would deny that experience with politics is relevant to political evaluation. The more experience and knowledge the better, and the more precise and thorough that knowledge the better; yet, are we really prepared to say that political knowledge and political experience are sufficient for evaluation? Do standards of evaluation simply grow from an accumulation of facts, however large? Surely not, for once having accumulated the facts we must ultimately *decide* to value X over Y or Y over Z. These decisions *can* be taken naïvely or arbitrarily, but they must be taken. Weldon himself finds it necessary to articulate certain standards, as we shall see below. The "model builders" of contemporary American political science find it necessary to postulate arbitrary (in the sense of "prescriptive definition") criteria for democracy, as noted in our introductory remarks.[17] The political scientist, learned though he may be, must leap beyond a mere accumulation of facts if he is to set up evaluative standards.[18] He may simply assert his own preferences, or he may prescribe standards for analytical purposes without recommending them; but if he seriously wishes to recommend his choice to someone else, he must tackle a problem that is not merely empirical but philosophical as well. Surely there *are* recommendations that a political scientist can make which are largely or purely empirical—means-to-ends recommendations of the type "if you want X, do Y." If, however, the political scientist wishes to make seriously an ultimate recommendation (e.g., democracy over authoritarianism), he must become a political philosopher to do so. Shifting the burden from professional philosophers to professional political scientists, as Weldon proposes, merely passes the problem along; it does not eliminate it.

Weldon feels compelled to remove the problem from philosophical consideration, because he is rightly convinced that neither metaphysics nor language analysis can deal with it. Thus, for him the problem of political evaluation is beyond the pale of philosophy, and if it is to be handled at all, it must be handled by someone other than the philosophers. It is at this point that our previous analysis enables us to see what Weldon is doing; why he is doing it; and finally, why his argument is unsatisfactory. We have argued that if justification in political philosophy is seen as a matter of deductive or inductive proof and if the alternative of deductive proof is found to be impossible, simple relativism or an attempt to escape relativism by turning to induction follows. We shall examine Weldon's argument very carefully and shall discover that, because he holds these presuppositions, Weldon attempts to explain the philosophical problem away. In doing so, he comes to an essentially relativist position that he tries to cover by an appeal to the wisdom of political researchers.

Weldon's argument is subtle and closely reasoned, and in order to do justice to it, we shall have to quote rather extensively. What I shall do is to quote roughly a page from *The Vocabulary of Politics,* and I shall interject remarks between Weldon's sentences where appropriate to our analysis. Remember that Weldon is here facing the problem of evaluating political institutions and therefore finds it necessary to erect a set of standards for evaluation. He begins by saying, "Now it is clear that 'Is the British legal system a good institution?', 'Is it superior to that of the U.S.S.R.?' are not philosophical questions."[19] I suggest that this assertion is anything but clear. On the contrary, it is quite clear that, if we take the words "good" and "superior" at all seriously, we shall ultimately have to accept a standard or standards in terms of which something is deemed "good," "superior," or "inferior." Empirical knowledge alone will not suffice if we are to escape relativism.[20] If such standards are to be justified, it will be necessary to engage in philosophy, and therefore Weldon's questions ultimately are philosophical questions, whether he is willing to admit it or not.

Weldon stresses the important empirical aspect of these questions but, unfortunately, tries to convince us that this is all that is involved. He continues, "Almost everyone would admit that we cannot even begin to answer them [the two questions] without a prolonged study of the way in which the two systems work both in theory and in practice." Quite so, but this does not eliminate the necessity of ultimately taking a philosophical stand. Weldon comes now to the crucial point: " 'Is communism superior to democracy?' looks easier but in fact it is not. Obviously all of us have not the time or the opportunity to go into such questions in detail, yet we cannot avoid taking sides, so what is to be done? *In fact the situation is not alarming.*" Here Weldon is trying to explain the problem away. When he tells us that the situation is not alarming, what he means is that it can be dealt with empirically without falling into relativism. I suggest that he is quite wrong about this —the situation *is* alarming, and Weldon's own analysis falls into relativism. Let us see where Weldon goes from here. "Each of us," he argues, "has his own tests, which are no doubt rough and crude, but they will serve their purpose, which is to check and confirm the conclusions of experts based on thorough research."[21] Surely this is a very peculiar way of eliminating the "alarming situation." What could be more relativistic than "each of us has our own tests"? Apparently, this relativism is supposed to be mitigated by the fact that the tests are only tentative and can be changed by the researches of "experts," as if it makes no difference whether we consult an American "expert" or a Soviet "expert." Weldon seemingly does not want to entertain the prospect of choosing between experts, perhaps because this kind of choice would in the final analysis have to be a philosophical choice if it were not to be simply arbitrary.

But Weldon does not leave the situation at this. He goes on to present his own "tests" and thus to show us that at least he is a democrat:[22]

> My own [tests] are approximately as follows:
> 1. Does the political system under consideration censor the reading of those who are subject to it and impose restrictions on teaching.
> 2. Does it maintain that any political or other principles are immutable and therefore beyond criticism?
> 3. Does it impose restrictions on the intercourse of its members with those who live under different systems?

These tests, we may agree, are rather good ones; but, as the British philosophers like to say, they tell us a good deal about Weldon but very little about the respective value of democracy or communism. Weldon, of course, is quite ready to admit this:[23]

> These are not final or conclusive tests, nor are they the only ones that matter, but any set of institutions which includes all these restrictions is *prima facie* a bad one, and the reason for claiming that it is bad is the presumption that those who are subject to it would reject it or escape from it if the restrictions were removed. I would therefore add:
> 4. Do the rulers of the association which has these institutions find most of their supporters among the illiterate, the uneducated, and the superstitious?

There are several ways of looking at this contention. First of all, if any credence is to be given to the researches of "experts" such as Erich Fromm, one may fairly doubt the generalization that "those who are subject to it would reject it or escape from it if the restrictions were removed."[24] Weldon tries to avoid this difficulty by eliminating "the illiterate, the uneducated, and the superstitious" à la John Stuart Mill—operationally, of course, an exceedingly difficult thing to do. However this may be, what Weldon is clearly doing is relying on the preferences of groups of people, and this is the important point. If people like it, it can be considered good. If not, it is *"prima facie bad."* Weldon's position is thus fundamentally relativist, and no amount of social science research is going to alter it.

In the last analysis, Weldon makes no pretense to anything more:[25]

> It does not follow that institutions which successfully pass all these tests are good. The absence of restrictions does not guarantee anything. But it seems to me important that people should make correct appraisals and it is certain that they cannot do this if they are kept in ignorance of the facts. *I must repeat however that this is my personal view, or prejudice if that word is preferred. It has nothing philosophical about it and may be rejected by anyone who disapproves of it.*

Weldon is thus doubly relativist, relying on his own "prejudice" to rely in turn on the prejudices of other people. We may, I think, fairly conclude that the situation is indeed "alarming," although perhaps not so alarming as the natural law theorists would have us believe.

It is advisable to examine Weldon's argument carefully, for his is a rather sophisticated presentation of a point of view "generally adopted today in the social sciences"[26] and held explicitly or implicitly by a great many political scientists. It is to this sort of view that a natural law–natural right theorist such as Professor Leo Strauss reacts so violently:[27]

> According to our social science, we can be or become wise in all matters of secondary importance, but we have to be resigned to utter ignorance in the most important respect: we cannot have any knowl-

edge regarding the ultimate principles of our choices, i.e., regarding their soundness or unsoundness; our ultimate principles have no other support than our arbitrary and hence blind preferences. We are then in the position of beings who are sane and sober when engaged in trivial business and who gamble like madmen when confronted with serious issues—retail sanity and wholesale madness. If our principles have no other support than our blind preferences, everything a man is willing to dare will be permissible. The contemporary rejection of natural right leads to nihilism—nay, it is identical with nihilism.

Strauss, refusing to be content with this allegedly nihilist position, is willing to accept the notions of classical antiquity according to which natural right can be inferred from an elaborate metaphysical apparatus. Between the views of Strauss, Hallowell, Walter Lippmann, and others and the view held by Weldon, John Dewey, Karl Popper, Arnold Brecht, and a great many social scientists lies the crucial issue of modern political thought. Either we shall have absolute standards by accepting the deductive thought model of traditional metaphysics, or we shall deny the validity of metaphysical deduction and thus deny the possibility of absolute standards. Weldon proposed a solution that we found unsatisfactory, and closer inspection will show the pragmatism of Dewey or the "piecemeal engineering" of Popper to be similarly unsatisfactory.[28] As suggested earlier, the key to the solution of this problem lies not in the differences between the two sides but in what they have in common. They share the notion that justification in political philosophy is a matter of deductive or inductive proof and that, in the absence of these alternatives, relativism alone remains. This is a mistake which we are now ready to analyze.

NOTES

[1] T. D. Weldon, *The Vocabulary of Politics* (Baltimore: Penguin Books, Inc., 1953), p. 97.

[2] *Ibid.*, pp. 97–98.

3 *Ibid.*, p. 86.

4 James Ward Smith, *Theme for Reason* (Princeton, N.J.: Princeton University Press, 1957), p. 17.

5 Weldon, *op. cit.*, pp. 192–193, as quoted in Smith, *op. cit.*, p. 17. (Italics added by Smith.)

6 See Smith, *op. cit.*, pp. 17–27.

7 John Dewey, to whom Smith also refers, is perhaps a much better one.

8 Weldon, *op. cit.*, pp. 14–15.

9 *Ibid.*, p. 160.

10 *Ibid.*, pp. 163–164.

11 Charles S. Hyneman, "Governmental Restraint of Expression: Tests for Evaluating Restrictive Acts" (unpublished paper, Department of Government, Indiana University, 1959), p. 2.

12 Weldon, *op. cit.*, p. 164.

13 *Ibid.*, pp. 168, 192.

14 *Ibid.*, pp. 178–179.

15 *Ibid.*, p. 172.

16 *Ibid.*, p. 175.

17 Cf., for example, Austin Ranney and Willmoore Kendall, *Democracy and the American Party System* (New York: Harcourt, Brace & World, Inc., 1956); Austin Ranney, *The Governing of Men* (New York: Holt, Rinehart and Winston, Inc., 1959); and Robert A. Dahl, *A Preface to Democratic Theory,* copyright 1956 by the University of Chicago (Chicago: University of Chicago Press).

18 Indeed, it has been argued, and to my mind convincingly, that the process of gathering facts itself is impossible without a prior theoretical, evaluative commitment. See Michael Polanyi, *Personal Knowledge: Towards a Post-critical Philosophy,* copyright 1958 by the University of Chicago (Chicago: University of Chicago Press); and Norwood Russell Hanson, *Patterns of Discovery: An Inquiry into the Conceptual Foundations of Science* (New York: Cambridge University Press, 1959).

19 Weldon, *op. cit.*, p. 175.

20 C. L. Stevenson's distinction between "attitudes" and "beliefs" may help to clarify this point. Cf. Stevenson's article "The Naure of Ethical Disagreement," in Milton K. Munitz (ed.), *A Modern Introduction to Ethics* (New York: The Free Press of Glencoe, Inc., 1958), pp. 547–552.

21 Weldon, *op. cit.*, pp. 175–176. (Italics added.)

22 *Ibid.*

23 *Ibid.* (Italics in original.)

24 Cf. Erich Fromm, *Escape from Freedom* (New York: Holt, Rinehart and Winston, Inc., 1941).

25 Weldon, *op. cit.*, p. 176. (Italics added.)

26 David Easton, *The Political System* (New York: Alfred A. Knopf, Inc., 1953), p. 221.

27 Leo Strauss, *Natural Right and History*. Copyright 1953 by the University of Chicago. (Chicago: University of Chicago Press), pp. 4–5.

28 Cf. Smith, *op. cit.*, pp. 15–28.

6

THE PROBLEM
RECONSIDERED

POLITICAL PHILOSOPHY
AS RECOMMENDATION

In the preceding pages we have found ourselves being highly critical of what are perhaps the two mainstreams of political thought. The course of our investigation revealed the serious inadequacy of two radically different approaches to the fundamental problems of politics. At this point, some words of qualification are perhaps in order. We must be quite clear about the fact that we have not rejected, or even wanted to reject, everything that Hallowell and Weldon have to say. On the contrary, the focus of our attack has in reality been quite narrow. The basic fact is simply that neither Weldon nor Hallowell has presented us with any genuine reasons for making an ultimate political commitment. In other words, although they both profess to justify democracy—Hallowell somewhat more explicitly than Weldon—neither of them really does it. If, as I think, part of Hallowell's argument is that Christians and/or people who adhere to a Greco–Judaeo-Christian set of moral precepts make good democrats, our analysis presents no special objection. This after all is not a philosophical but an empirical point, logically parallel to the contention that a functioning democracy requires a large middle class. Likewise, in so far as Weldon is an advocate of experience with politics and favors empirical study, we have no quarrel with him. Our analysis is misunderstood if it is read either as an attack on religion or as an attack on a scientific political science. It may be an attack on theology, but not on religion. It is an attack on "scientific

value relativism," to use Brecht's phrase,[1] but it is not an attack
on the scientific study of politics. We do not argue for an end to
prayer or statistics, but simply for recognition of the fact that
neither of these methods can solve the problems of political
philosophy.

Just how are the problems of political philosophy to be
solved? We quoted Hallowell and Weldon not so much for the
virtues or vices of their respective expositions as for the general
points of view they represent. We realized more than that
Hallowell and Weldon failed to justify democracy; we saw
that political philosophy will not work on either a deductive
or an inductive model. Above all, we saw that political philosophy is misconceived as a search for proofs. If this is so, it will
be necessary to tear ourselves loose from presuppositions, to
reorient our thinking, and to reconsider the fundamental
nature or, if you will, the logic of political philosophy.

Ordinarily, political philosophy as studied in American universities consists in the examination of the teachings of a particular political philosopher or a number of political philosophers. The student is obliged to examine the writings of a
thinker with an eye to the fundamental premises of his argument, his differences with prior and subsequent writers, his
specific conclusions, and the consistency of his argument. Thus
we come to see Plato as deducing his republic from a theory of
ideal forms. We learn that Hobbes rooted his political conceptions in a notion of the depravity of man, that Bentham
recommended a standard for legislation on the basis of a theory
of ethical hedonism, etc. Now there is nothing wrong with this
method, unless this elaborate investigation clouds our minds
to the basic purpose of every political philosopher of any merit.
That purpose is in some respects obvious, but its implications
are profound. Political philosophy—whether in the hands of
Plato, Hobbes, Mill, or Marx—is basically a recommendation
or set of recommendations on how men should conduct politics. These are not ordinarily recommendations casually advanced to meet a specific problem, but recommendations that

are *intended* to be valid for all time. Nevertheless, they *are* recommendations; therefore the logic of political philosophy is the logic of recommendation. By "logic of recommendation" I do not refer to a unique logical system but rather to the analysis of the use of recommendations and what is involved in justifying them.

As remarked above, this is in a sense all very obvious; but, as with a good many other obvious statements, we have to learn to take it seriously. Perhaps an example or two will help us to see that my statement on the recommendatory character of political philosophy is not so obvious as it may seem. In our introductory remarks we quoted at some length from Daniel J. Boorstin's attack on the notion of a philosophy of democracy in his book *The Genius of American Politics.* Boorstin speaks of "the un-American demand for a philosophy of democracy." He argues that advocates of a philosophy of democracy "are among our most dangerous friends" who would try to fill "the *sanctum sanctorum* of national belief," which Boorstin says is empty, with "their own graven image, their own ass's head, and say that is what belonged there all the time." He further argues that we Americans should not ask other countries "to adopt our 'philosophy' because we have no philosophy which can be exported."[2] Apparently, for Boorstin the writings of Jefferson, Madison, and Hamilton are something other than political philosophy. Happily the countless Europeans, Asians, and Africans—not to mention subsequent generations of Ameri͵ cans—who have taken inspiration from these writings have not been inclined to disregard them on this account.

While there are many good things about Boorstin's book, his denigration of political philosophy is not one of them. The key to Boorstin's confusion is his conception of the nature of political philosophy. Let us look carefully at his first paragraph:[3]

> The genius of American democracy comes not from any special virtue of the American people but from the unprecedented opportunities of this continent and from a peculiar and unrepeatable com-

bination of historical circumstances. These circumstances have given our institutions their character and their virtues. The very same facts which explain these virtues, explain also *our inability to make a "philosophy" of them. They explain our lack of interest in political theory, and why we are doomed to failure in any attempt to sum up our way of life in slogans and dogmas. They explain, therefore, why we have nothing in the line of a theory that can be exported to other peoples of the world.*

Unless I misread this paragraph, part of what is being said is that " 'philosophy' cum political theory" equals "slogans and dogmas." Boorstin later says that political theory has "been primarily interested in discovering and systematizing general truths about society, regardless of time and place" and that these theories have been used as "a blueprint for remaking society." Boorstin sees political philosophy as identical with a dogmatic prescription of ends or goals for a society, and he rightly objects to traditional European political philosophy. "The European concept of a political community is of a group oriented toward fulfilling an explict philosophy; political life there is the *world of ends and absolutes.*"[4] "The characteristic tyrannies of our age—nazism, fascism, and communism," he says elsewhere, " . . . justify their outrages because their 'philosophies' require them."[5] Boorstin very correctly condemns political philosophy which dogmatically prescribes social ends and which is used to "justify" tyranny, but he is in error with his apparent conclusion that this kind of enterprise constitutes the very *definition* of political philosophy.

I suggest that what Boorstin is objecting to is what we have called "deductive absolutism," and he makes the mistake of seeing political philosophy *as* deductive absolutism. What he does not take seriously enough is the rather obvious notion that political philosophy is always basically a set of general recommendations about politics. If he saw the true import of this characterization, how could he describe the American situation in terms of "our refusal to make our society into the graven image of any man's political philosophy."[6] Surely if we were talking in terms of recommendation, Locke or Madison or Jefferson, or all three together, would be fine candidates. However, since none of them were deductive absolutists in any genuine sense, they consequently do not fit Boorstin's notion of a "builder of graven images." What he quite rightly objects to are the Hallowells, who would fill the *sanctum sanctorum* of our national belief with classical realism or some other "graven image." But it is simply a mistake to maintain that political philosophizing *means* building graven images.

The tendency to identify political philosophy with deductive absolutism is widespread both among its adherents and among its opponents, as we saw in our discussion of Hallowell and Weldon and now, in a less explicit way, in Boorstin. Part of what we saw in our analysis of Hallowell was that the metaphysical, deductive apparatus which has so often accompanied political philosophizing is in large part irrelevant window dressing; that is, it merely provides a linguistic recipe for making political recommendations. Thus, it is simply a mistake to look at political philosophy in terms of the logical model of deduction. For different but equally persuasive reasons, it is an error to pattern this enterprise on the model of induction. Deducing and inducing will surely enter into any political philosophy, but they will always be subordinate parts. The major direction of political philosophy is of a logically different character—it is recommendatory.

I remarked earlier that the implications of this change of emphasis, this different way of looking at political philosophy, were profound. This statement was intended quite seriously, for so far as our problem of justifying democracy is concerned it means that we must stop looking for better deductions or inductions and start looking for recommendations. Just what is involved here is by no means easy to comprehend. What we shall have to do is to investigate the logic of recommendation, a task that cannot be accomplished without becoming enmeshed in one of the most difficult problems of modern philosophy. The problem, stated in its awesome simplicity, is merely this—what does it mean to be rational? There is a sense in which this problem, at least in the way in which I want to focus upon it, is a distinctively modern one. Under the decisive influence of the early work of Wittgenstein,[7] modern philosophy has perhaps been more explicit about the limits of rationality than has any earlier period. Gustav Bergmann, in attempting to summarize the basic tenets of logical positivism, lays the groundwork for us:[8]

> . . . *as long as one sticks to cautious generalities* all Logical Positivists could still agree that they (a) hold Humean views on causality and induction; (b) insist on the tautological nature of logical and mathematical truths; (c) conceive of philosophy as logical analysis, i.e., as a clarification of the language which we speak in everyday life; and (d) that such analysis leads to the "rejection of metaphysics" in the sense that, e.g., the points at dispute among the *traditional* forms of idealism, realism, and phenomenalism could not even be stated, or, at least not be stated in their original intent, in a properly clarified language.

These, of course, are essentially the precepts held by Weldon in his attack on metaphysics in political philosophy and are in large part the notions we have followed in our own analysis.

What all this indicates about the limits of rationality may not, however, be immediately apparent. The focus of logical positivism is on the analysis of language, and our question thus recurs in this form: what kinds of statements are rational? A. J. Ayer, in his provocative little book *Language, Truth and Logic,*[9] which as Bergmann remarks has almost the status of a text,[10] addresses the problem somewhat more specifically:[11]

> To test whether a sentence expresses a genuine empirical hypothesis, I adopt what may be called a modified verification principle. For I require of an empirical hypothesis, not indeed that it should be conclusively verifiable, but that *some possible sense-experience should be relevant to the determination of its truth or falsehood.* If a putative proposition fails to satisfy this principle, and is not a *tautology,* then I hold that it is metaphysical, and that, being metaphysical, it is neither true nor false but *literally senseless.*

What we are being given here is something very like a definition of what it means to talk sense. Actually, we are being told
that a meaningful statement must either be hypothesis subject
to empirical verification or analytic truth. If it is neither of
these, it is "literally senseless." As Ayer again expresses it later,
"And as tautologies and empirical hypotheses form the entire
class of significant propositions, we are justified in concluding
that all metaphysical assertions are nonsensical."[12] This is slip-
pery ground, and we shall have to be careful about what we
say. "Senseless" and "nonsensical" are very strong words, and
one may wonder precisely what Ayer means by them. One
thing we can be certain of: Ayer maintains that it makes no
sense to say of a traditional metaphysical proposition (e.g., "the
universe is an all-encompassing spirit") that it is true or false.
Since this statement is neither analytic (i.e., tautologous) nor
subject to verification by sense data, it cannot be said to be true
or false; thus it is *empirically* or, as is sometimes said, *cogni-
tively* meaningless. Is this the same as saying that this statement
and others like it are *not rational?*

Let us defer the answer to this question for a moment so
that we may consider the kind of statement significant to our
investigation, namely, the recommendatory statement. Suppose that we were to present Ayer with the recommendation
"we ought to adopt democracy." What would he say about it?
Quite clearly, it is neither analytic nor subject to verification
by sense data; presumably, therefore, it must be "literally
senseless." Ayer is not content, however, to leave it at this,
for he has his own special way of dealing with evaluative statements. A purely evaluative statement, of course, cannot have
cognitive meaning, because it does not meet either of the two
tests, but it does have emotive meaning; that is, the speaker
uses it to express his own feeling, and the listener if properly
oriented may be able to understand what feeling the speaker is
expressing. "Literally senseless" in this context does not mean,
therefore, that an evaluative statement is equivalent to "blah
goo blah aba"—it is not meaningless in the sense that it is

gibberish. However, for Ayer there is no possibility of determining the rightness or wrongness of an evaluative statement:[13]

> We can now see why it is impossible to find a criterion for determining the validity of ethical judgements. It is not because they have an "absolute" validity which is mysteriously independent of ordinary sense-experience, but because they have no objective validity whatsoever. If a sentence makes no statement at all, there is obviously no sense in asking whether what it says is true or false. And we have seen that sentences which simply express moral judgements do not say anything [because they are neither tautologous or empirically verifiable]. They are pure expressions of feeling and as such do not come under the category of truth or falsehood. They are unverifiable for the same reason as a cry of pain or a word of command is unverifiable—because they do not express genuine propositions.

"We ought to adopt democracy" would thus be said to be logically equivalent to "*I feel* that we ought to adopt democracy" or, more precisely according to Ayer's analysis, to "Democracy! ! !"—"where the shape and thickness of the exclamation marks show, by a suitable convention, that a special sort of moral [approval] is the feeling which is being expressed."[14]

Is it rational to say that we ought to adopt democracy? I do not pretend to know how Ayer would answer this question, and in any case it is not very important. What is important for our purposes is to see the stultifying effect that these pronouncements have had on social and political philosophy. In the introductory chapter we noted Morton White's remark that the effect has been very unfortunate within philosophy itself, and I should say that it has been even more unfortunate in social and political science. These are substantially the views that David Easton correctly tells us are "generally adopted today in the social sciences"—if not explicitly then implicitly. The scientific political scientist shies away from evaluative statements and ultimate recommendations, almost as if to make such "commitments" were to violate some primitive taboo. If a recommendation is at its core an emotive ejaculation, so the argument runs, then there is no way of rationally choosing between recommendations. If you like it, you like it. If you do not like it, you do not like it. A great deal can be said about why certain people like it and why others do not; but when it comes to making an ultimate recommendation himself, the political scientist *qua* political scientist will have none of it.

As remarked earlier, there is a sense in which this development is a distinctively modern one. Few philosophers before the logical positivists have been so explicit about imputing a superior status to empirical hypotheses and analytic statements. As is nearly always the case, however, Wittgenstein and the others were making explicit what had long been implicit in the Western philosophical tradition. As Wittgenstein himself once phrased it, "The problems are solved, not by giving new information, but by arranging what we have always known."[15] In so far as empirical hypotheses are associated with the logical model of induction and analytic statements with deduction—and the association is of course intimate—the positivist thesis is another way of recognizing the superior status of induction and deduction, a superiority long taken for granted by philosophers and laymen alike. It is small wonder then that moderns such as Hallowell and Weldon, when faced with the problem of ultimate recommendation, turn on the one hand to deduction as a logical model and on the other to a rather loose brand of induction.

Modern philosophy has thus reinforced and made more explicit the notion that rational answers must be arrived at by deduction or induction. Consequently, it is the problem of "rationality" that we shall have to review. As Professor Smith has expressed it:[16]

> Perhaps nothing so confines and encumbers our ways of approaching philosophical questions as our tendency to conceive of the demands of rationality on inadequate standard models. No need is more pressing in the present scene than the need for reinterpreting what we mean by "rational opinion." We persist in operating in terms of two ideal models of rationality: on the one hand, the model of logico-

mathematical deduction; on the other hand, the model of piecemeal inductive engineering. We feel that we are being rational only to the extent that we confine ourselves to the enunciation either of demonstrated theorems within deductive systems or of empirical hypotheses which sheer weight of evidence will tend to confirm or confute. Though we may be aware that we cannot confine ourselves to these two ideal ways of talking, we continue to approach intellectual problems as though doing anything else is either careless or at best an unfortunate necessity. Reason is tacitly conceded to be a faculty for seeing everything in system; if an opinion can be shown to be a theorem deducible from axioms it is conceded to be a rational opinion, if it can be shown to be an hypothesis made probable by experimental evidence it is conceded to be rational; opinions of any other sort are (whether frowned upon or hailed) conceived to be somehow not rational.

But what we have seen in our examination of Hallowell and Weldon is that neither of the two standard models of rationality will satisfy in political philosophy. Ultimate political recommendations are neither empirical hypotheses nor theorems in a deductive system. While it is quite true that they cannot therefore be regarded as either true or false, it does not follow as Ayer seems to think that one is as "senseless" as another. If, as we have alleged, political philosophy is a matter of recommendation, we must be able to discriminate among recommendations; above all, we must be able to justify democracy in terms of the logic of recommendation.

For all this our justification will be no less rational, for rationality consists in deciding wisely in terms of the context of the decision. If a decision in favor of democracy cannot be made on the basis of *proof* of either variety, this is not to say that it cannot be made rationally. We must learn.[17]

> . . . to move more boldly in that vast middle ground which stretches between theorem-deriving and experimental induction. A sensible man must be tenacious of his opinions in many contexts where "proof," either deductive or inductive, is out of the question. . . . There is a sense of certainty which is far from logical and yet equally far from the tentativeness customarily assigned to piecemeal prediction of matters of fact. There are "musts" in our intellectual life which

are neither the "musts" of logic nor the "musts" of incontrovertible evidence. . . . Opinions must be justified in context; and if there is any coerciveness about an opinion the character of that coerciveness must be described in context and in detail.

THE NATURE OF RECOMMENDATION

What does it mean to say that political philosophy is recommendation? On the basis of what has been said so far, the implications of this contention are not yet clear. We may take a statement such as "we ought to adopt democracy" and readily see its recommendatory character, but the history of political philosophy is not replete with statements of this kind. A good many of what would likely be classified as the important statements of political philosophy do not appear as explicit "ought" statements at all; on the contrary, they seem to be statements of fact. Such crucial statements as " . . . when each order—tradesman, Auxiliary, Guardian—keeps to its own proper business in the commonwealth and does its own work, that is justice and what makes a good society," "All men by nature are equal," and "The mode of production of the material means of existence conditions the whole process of social, political, and intellectual life" seem not to be recommendations but observations on the way the world is. I believe it is possible to show, however, that they are better understood as recommendations. While we are inclined to follow the dictates of grammar and hence to treat these remarks as statements of fact that may be true or false, we are wrong in this assumption, and we shall continue to be misled as long as we persist in reading them in these terms. Only when we can see them for what they are—recommendations—shall we be able to make headway in political philosophy.

Statements which *grammatically* appear to state facts but which *logically* make recommendations are by no means pecul-

iar to political philosophy. In order to see what is involved in
these profoundly serious and important statements in political
philosophy, I propose that we begin by examining a much less
serious and less important remark we frequently make in ordinary conversation.[18] Let us have a careful look at that familiar cliché "What you don't know won't hurt you." Surely
this has all the characteristics of a statement of fact. The verbs
are ordinary indicatives as in any statement of fact. Still, how
would we react if we addressed this remark to a friend and he
began to elaborately demonstrate that it was neither an empirical hypothesis which could be confirmed by reference to evidence nor a theorem which can be deduced from a set of axioms? We would probably think that he had misunderstood
what we said, and we might perhaps repeat the remark, hoping
that its import would sink in.

Of course, it is *possible* to read this statement as an empirical
hypothesis or as an analytic statement. As an empirical hypothesis it is so obviously false as to be downright stupid.
"What we do not know" does hurt us frequently and might
conceivably end our lives at any time. Similarly, it is easy
enough to turn this statement into an analytic proposition by
defining its terms in certain ways. Suppose, for example, that
"what you know" is taken to mean "anything that you are
aware of" and that "hurt you" means "to have a certain kind of
awareness." Thus, our statement will turn out to mean "What
you are not aware of you are not aware of." This is obviously
true, but it is trivial and, most importantly, not what we
meant.

The old cliché seems to fail the tests of rationality. As an empirical statement it is absurd, and as a tautology it is trivial.
If, as we have implied, it is something else, it must be "literally
senseless"; or to put it more benevolently, it may have "emotive" meaning. But this will not do. We do mean something
by "What you don't know won't hurt you," and to say that
the meaning is "emotive" is so general a description that it
clarifies nothing. More than this, it may be completely mis-

leading, for I may be saying something quite sensible that has very little to do with my passions. If you and I were sitting together on an airplane and you began to speculate that someone aboard might be concealing a bomb, I might quite sensibly say "What you don't know won't hurt you." Clearly, I do not mean by this that, if someone aboard does have a bomb, the fact that you do not know about it will prevent it from hurting you. In other words, the statement is not intended as an empirical hypothesis. What I mean to say is "Relax! Stop worrying!" I am offering a recommendation, a piece of advice. Whether or not it is a *good* recommendation will depend on whether or not there is a bomb aboard, but this has nothing whatsoever to do with whether or not "What you don't know won't hurt you" is true or false. A recommendation is related to the context in which it is given—it may in context be good or bad, appropriate or inappropriate; but we cannot determine the validity of a recommendation by testing it for truth or falsity.

We have seen that the old cliché, while put in the indicative mood, is misunderstood as a statement of fact. Let us turn now to Locke's solemn and important statement "All men by nature are equal." Does it make sense to treat this indicative as a statement of fact? Can we imagine that Locke intended to present us with a straightforward empirical hypothesis? Surely he is not trying to tell us that some men are not geniuses and some morons, that some are not rich and others poor. Is he on the other hand envincing a tautology? He could, of course, be saying that "All men are by nature men," just as all cats are by nature cats or all trees are by nature trees. Again the statement seems to be absurd as an empirical hypothesis and trivial as a tautology. If I am right, the fundamental point of Locke's statement is this: in certain contexts all men ought to behave as if they were the equal of any other man. Here is Locke himself on this point:[19]

> Though I have said above "that all men by nature are equal," I cannot be supposed to understand all sorts of equality. Age or virtue may give men a just precedency; excellency of parts and merit may

place others above the common level; birth may subject some, and alliance or benefits others, to pay an observance to those whom nature, gratitude or other respects may have made it due; and yet all this consists with the equality which all men are in, in respect of jurisdiction or dominion one over another, which was the equality I there spoke of as proper to the business in hand, being that equal right that every man hath to his natural freedom, without being subjected to the will or authority of any other man.

Let us be quite clear about this. Locke's remarks here, taken at face value, do not say quite what I have said they say. I argued that according to Locke all men *ought* to behave in a certain way in a certain context, but Locke himself seems to be saying that in this certain context all men *are* this way. What we seem to be saying here is that Locke did not quite understand what he was doing. Presumptuous as this suggestion may sound, I think it is essentially correct. Here the fact that Locke was a seventeenth-century Englishman rather than a twentieth-century Englishman is crucial. Locke would probably have imagined that he could supply *proof* for this "statement of fact" (now qualified to read something like "In certain respects all men are by nature equal"), when in truth no *proof* is available. It cannot be *proved* as an empirical hypothesis, because no empirical evidence is relevant to its confirmation or confutation—it is just *not* an empirical hypothesis! Likewise, it cannot be *proved* by deducing it from some grand statement such as "All men are rational" for all the reasons that we discussed earlier. What we have before us is a statement that "When it comes to the question of the dominance of one man over another, all men are equal"; and what "All men are equal" means in this context is that no man should be allowed to dominate another without his consent. We have no statement of fact that can be *proved;* we have a recommendation that has to be *justified.*

When Plato defined justice, whatever he may have thought or however the grammar may appear, he was not stating a fact; he was telling us that society *should* be organized in this particular way. Perhaps no one in the history of Western thought was as explicitly enthusiastic about facts as was Karl Marx; yet when he postulated his fundamental premise that the means of production is the controlling force in history, he was not stating a fact. I do not mean here that what he said is empirically false, although it certainly is. What I do mean is that the setting forth of additional facts is irrelevant to his contention and is treated as such by any Marxist. If Marx and the Marxists were presenting us with an empirical generalization, a single counter instance would shatter the whole edifice. What Marx is really telling us is that this is the way we *should* look at the world if we are to be saved. It is no accident nor, as is sometimes said, is it inconsistent with his views that Marx should have proclaimed, "The philosophers have only *interpreted* the world; the point however is to *change* it." Marx was recommending and he knew it, but he made the mistake of imagining that his recommendations could be *proved* by reference to the facts of history.[20]

Part of what is wrong with the political philosophies of Plato and Marx is that neither of them completely faced the fact that they *were* recommending and *were not* stating facts. I do not mean to say that there are no factual statements in Plato or Marx but only that their major premises, which they imagined to be factual, were in reality very large recommendations concerning the way in which the world should be approached. Both of them were misled into attempting the logically impossible task of leaping from a limited quantity of empirical evidence (with regard to generalizations, empirical evidence is always limited) to generalized statements about the way the world "is," and then—to pile mistake upon mistake—into attempting the equally impossible task of deducing recommendations from them. Apparently on the basis of his study of geometry, Plato argued that, just as every actual triangle is an imperfect copy of an ideal triangle, so every actual chair is an imperfect copy of an ideal chair, every actual state is an imperfect copy of an ideal state. For Plato this is the *proper* way of looking at the world. Similarly, Marx, observing that a change in the means of production brought about the change from feudalism to capitalism (and of course, other comparable observations), concluded that *all* change is a consequence of changes in the means of production. It is news to no one that Marx saw this as *the* key to history, the *proper* way of looking at the world. Thus, not only did Plato and Marx recommend at the conclusion of their arguments, but they were recommending from the very beginning. They were, as we saw earlier, stating their recommendations in the highly general language of a *Weltanschauung*.[21]

Another, and extremely significant, way of characterizing the deficiencies of Plato and Marx as political philosophers is this: their theories fail as absolutely general and absolutely binding recommendations. Neither Plato nor Marx faced the fact that they were recommending in our sense of the term. Had they done so, they might have seen as we now can that, while their recommendations might be very good and very helpful in some contexts, there is no reason to suppose they are good in every context. It is helpful to see reality as an imperfect copy of an ideal form in some contexts. This is what Newton did when he posited the law of the inverse squares. Likewise, it is helpful to see economics as *a* or even *the* causal factor in some contexts, as when we examine the behavior of some pressure groups. But such recommendations may be ridiculous when the biologist studies a mutant form of some creature, or when one examines the behavior of Albert Schweitzer. Neither of these theories can be accepted as absolutely general and absolutely binding recommendations, because we cannot know that they are accurate.

We are beginning to focus upon what seems to me to be the crucial question in political philosophy. If, as we have argued, the essential character of political philosophy is recommendatory, the important question is this: is there anything that will function as an absolutely general and absolutely binding rec-

ommendation in political philosophy? If there is such a recommendation, it and it alone will serve to justify our ultimate
political choices. But what can we mean by the claim that a
recommendation is general and binding? What, first of all,
could we mean by saying that a recommendation is binding?
Let us return for a moment to "What you don't know won't
hurt you." We might want to say that in certain contexts this
simply *is* a good recommendation, and in that sense it is binding. For example, if a friend begins to speculate that there
might at this moment be a man in a local tavern rapidly becoming more and more drunk who will later in the evening
smash into our friend's parked car causing him untold misery
and expense, we might say that "What you don't know won't
hurt you" *is* a good recommendation in this context. Surely,
however, there is nothing to be said for the cliché as a generalization. Addressed to a man who has cancer of the liver but
does not know it, it might be the worst possible recommendation. Taken alone and out of context the cliché is overgeneral
as a recommendation, but this is not to say that it is false as an
empirical hypothesis. Here we are not treating it as a hypothesis; we are treating it as a recommendation, and as such it is too
general.[22]

Much the same can be said for "All men are by nature
equal." We may agree with Locke that when dealing with the
problem of the domination of one man over another it just
is a good recommendation. We may want to expand our argument by saying that the divine right of kings, racial elitism,
and any other notion which seeks to demonstrate the natural
superiority of some are a lot of metaphysical hogwash and
should be disregarded. On the other hand, when it comes to
setting up an educational system or admitting men to the practice of medicine, we may want to argue that "All men are by
nature equal" should not be taken very seriously. As a recommendation Locke's phrase, as he himself saw, is too general.

One of the factors we should recognize is that the question typically asked about notable statements in political phi-

losophy is wholly inappropriate. It is beside the point to ask of "All men are by nature equal" whether it is true. The proper question here is, "In what contexts does it constitute a good recommendation?" There is a great deal of talk in the history of political thought about *"the* nature of man." And there is a great deal of discussion in seminars on political philosophy as to whether this or that conception of the nature of man is *true.* This is a discussion of the wrong question. James Ward Smith sums up the argument with considerable clarity:[23]

> Most of the giants of political theory are giants because they have caught hold of some genuine insight into the ways of mankind. They have consequently given advice which has been relevant, important, and moving. Unfortunately they overstate their advice in capsule propositional form. In that form it crystallizes in the traditions of academic debate, and therefore we argue about the wrong thing. Consider some examples:
>
> Locke and Rousseau, each in his own way, proclaimed that man is naturally good. When you study what they have to say in full and in the contexts of the problems with which they were faced, it is clear enough that they were saying something which within limits is sound and important. Essentially they were recommending that social institutions should be thought of as instruments through which men can achieve what they want. Machiavelli said that men were selfish and acquisitive; Hobbes said that they are governed by the instinct of self-preservation; the Puritans said bluntly that men are depraved. Again, if you study what they have to say in full and in the contexts of the problems with which they were concerned, it is clear enough that these men too were saying something which within limits is sound and important. Essentially they were recommending that social institutions must be so set up that individuals cannot use authority to satisfy their own interests at the expense of the general interest.
>
> Surely, abstract debate concerning whether *the* nature of man is good or depraved is a way of sidestepping rather than solving the fundamental question, which is: Under what conditions do you advise men to assert their interests and desires, and under what conditions do you advise men to suppress those interests and desires?

Thus, one of the important tasks of students of politics is to assess the appropriateness of recommendations to certain contexts. Scientific political science receives what is probably its best support from this notion. How, it is asked, can we possibly assess the appropriateness of recommendations to a particular context without a thorough and correct knowledge of that context? The answer is that we cannot. If scientific methods provide, as I think they do, the best means—in a sense the only means—of understanding a political situation, then surely they are to be encouraged. In this context Weldon's comment is very appropriate; "In fact the crucial question which needs to be answered before we set out to reform other peoples' institutions is . . . 'Do we know enough about the facts to be qualified to give helpful advice in this case?', and it should be remembered that the revelant facts include the traditions, history, geographical conditions, education, and customary standard of living of the people concerned."[24] Limited recommendation does require knowledge of contexts, that is, political situations; and if this is to be acquired by statistical correlation, interviews, game theory, deductive models, or whatever, it should not be maligned by the political philosopher but encouraged by him. In the context of limited recommendation, Weldon's call for experience with politics and for empirical study makes perfect sense.

But—and this is the all important but—ultimate political choices are not limited to certain contexts; they are to be binding in any context whatsoever, and this poses a need that empirical study cannot meet. What we shall say about a limited recommendation even after we know the context thoroughly will in part depend on basic commitments applying to any context. If we are seriously concerned about what means will prevent tyranny, we shall first have to decide that the prevention of tyranny *is* an important concern, we shall have to decide that government and politics are subjects to be thought of seriously. We must take *some* recommendations as absolutely general and absolutely binding to operate at all. The justification of an ultimate political commitment—this is our problem.

NOTES

1 Arnold Brecht, *Political Theory: The Foundations of Twentieth Century Political Thought* (Princeton, N.J.: Princeton University Press, 1959), p. 117ff.

2 Daniel J. Boorstin, *The Genius of American Politics*. Copyright 1953 by the University of Chicago. (Chicago: University of Chicago Press), pp. 1, 184–185.

3 *Ibid.*, p. 1. (Italics added.)

4 *Ibid.*, pp. 2–3, 184. (Italics added.)

5 *Ibid.*, p. 3.

6 *Ibid.*

7 Ludwig Wittgenstein, *Tractatus Logico-Philosophicus* (London: Routledge & Kegan Paul Ltd., 1922).

8 Gustav Bergmann, *The Metaphysics of Logical Positivism* (New York: David McKay Company, Inc., 1954), p. 2. (Italics in original.)

9 A. J. Ayer, *Language, Truth and Logic*. Reprinted through permission by Dover Publications, New York 14, N.Y., 1953.

10 Bergmann, *op. cit.*, p. 3.

11 Ayer, *op. cit.*, p. 31. (Italics added.)

12 *Ibid.*, p. 41.

13 *Ibid.*, pp. 108–109.

14 *Ibid.*, p. 107.

15 Ludwig Wittgenstein, *Philosophical Investigations* (New York: The Macmillan Company, 1953), No. 109, p. 47: "Die Probleme werden gelöst, nicht durch Beibringen neuer Erfahrung, sondren durch Zusammenstellung des längst Bekannten."

16 James Ward Smith, *Theme for Reason* (Princeton, N.J.: Princeton University Press, 1957), p. 6.

17 *Ibid.*, p. 5.

18 What I shall have to say here essentially follows the keen analysis of Smith, *op. cit.*, pp. 49–59.

19 John Locke, *The Second Treatise of Civil Government*, chap. VI, par. 3.

20 Cf. Isaiah Berlin, *Historical Inevitability* (New York: Oxford University Press, 1954).

21 Our earlier analysis of deductive absolutism is, of course, extremely relevant here.

22 Smith, *op. cit.*, pp. 51–52.

23 *Ibid.*, pp. 54–55. (Italics in original.)

24 T. D. Weldon, *The Vocabulary of Politics* (Baltimore: Penguin Books, Inc., 1953), pp. 178–79.

7

TOWARD A SOLUTION

THE PROBLEM OF ANALYSIS

"Only by seeing what *cannot* be done can we see what *can* be done." These were the words which I used to preface our examination of various attempts to justify democracy. I call attention to this phrase again because it sets the tone for this entire analysis. "The history of philosophy is in large degree a record of blunders and mistakes. There is a small kernel of truth in the familiar claim that philosophy 'gets nowhere'."[1] Only by looking carefully at prior attempts to justify democracy, and by seeing the mistakes, are we able to move off in what seems to be a more sensible direction. We critically examine philosophical writings on democracy not to divine what the authors "really meant" but to clarify our own problem. As D. J. O'Conner so aptly puts it, "When we read philosophy, we are not going to an authority for information but to the product of a lively mind which will stimulate us to philosophize for ourselves."[2] We concentrate on past mistakes in order to set our own thinking right. To be critical is a large part of what it means to be philosophical.[3]

Modern analytic philosophers are prone to say that philosophy consists in the clarification of concepts.[4] This statement should be taken seriously, but not too seriously. It should be taken seriously to the extent that we should not expect a philosophical advance to be something utterly novel, the likes of which we have never heard before. In so far as philosophy is the clarification of concepts, it is an edifice built on a critique of what has gone before; a genuine advance is *not* likely to be a wholly new vocabulary or the postulation of an absolutely novel set of problems but rather a change of focus or of emphasis with respect to traditional problems, accompanied by a new perspective on the old vocabulary. As Kant warns us,[5]

> There are scholarly men to whom the history of philosophy (both ancient and modern) is philosophy itself. . . . They must wait till those who endeavor to draw from the fountain of reason itself have completed their work; it will then be the turn of these scholars to inform the world of what has been done. Unfortunately, nothing can be said which, in their opinion, has not been said before, and truly the same prophecy applies to all future time; for since the human reason has for many centuries speculated upon innumerable objects in various ways, it is hardly to be expected that we should not be able to discover analogies for every new idea among the old sayings of past ages.

But, as Kant implies, to see an analogy is not necessarily to see an identity.

It is, however, a mistake to imagine that a clarification of concepts can ever be *merely* that.[6] The notion that philosophy is "wholly critical," merely concerned with the analysis and clarification of language and concepts, has wide circulation.[7] This notion stems from the conviction that philosophy is properly conceived as the handmaiden of science. According to this view, the gathering of knowledge about the world is wholly the concern of science; philosophy can only assist science by clarifying its statements and by clearing away linguistic conundrums. (Recall Weldon's statement that political philosophy should clarify the concepts of political science.) Science, it is alleged, proceeds by dispassionate induction and deduction, while philosophy puts these procedures to the test of logic. As a consequence of all this, the attempts of traditional philosophy to solve real world problems are dismissed as metaphysical nonsense. It is precisely these attempts that Ayer chooses the phrase "literally senseless" to deal with. Thus it is that we are led to believe there is an unbridgeable gap between "problem solving in the grand tradition" and "analysis." Analysis is conceived as "mere" analysis; it does not deal with the problems of the grand tradition. In political science we see the very same gap, this time between "problem solving in the grand tradition" and "scientific political science." One of the most celebrated books in political science begins by announcing the existence of this gap in unequivocal terms:[8]

> The study of politics is the study of influence and the influential. The science of politics states conditions; the philosophy of politics justifies preferences. This book, *restricted to political analysis,* declares no preferences. It states conditions.

Hundreds of people after having read or heard a statement such as this have made the essentially trite remark that no one can exclude value judgments from his exposition. This is a *psychological* comment on the fallible character of the human mind, and Lasswell and anyone who sympathizes with him can justifiably shrug it off as being beside the point. We are, they may say, dealing with an ideal; of course, we are only human and thus may not reach the ideal. Nevertheless, this objection does not damage the ideal in principle.

But the ideal itself is illusory! The real objection is a logical one, which consists in this: no one can say anything, recognize anything, understand anything without committing himself to a theoretical apparatus. And this theoretical apparatus is not something which can be *proved.* If Lasswell thinks—of course, I do not know what he thinks, but only what he says—that he is *merely* analyzing, he is wrong. There is no such thing as *mere* analysis in political science or in philosophy or in science as a whole. The serious use of the tools of logical and scientific analysis commits one to a certain view of the world. It is for just this reason that a comment on scientific political science such as the following by a "problem solver in the grand tradition," Professor Leo Strauss, bites so hard:[9]

> . . . contemporary social scientists . . . teach that every society rests, in the last analysis, on specific values or on specific myths, i.e., on assumptions which are not evidently superior or preferable to any alternative assumptions. They imply, therefore, that social science reveals and stresses the arbitrary character of the basic assumptions

underlying any given society; social science desires to be "objective" and "undogmatic." They fail to see, however, that this state of things creates a tension between the requirements of social science (knowledge of the truth and teaching of the truth) and the requirements of society (whole-hearted acceptance of the principles of society): if I know that the principles of liberal democracy are not intrinsically superior to the principles of communism or fascism, I am incapable of whole-hearted commitment to liberal democracy.

Thus, the political scientist is in the oddly paradoxical situation of praising political consensus and at the same time helping to break it down. It is precisely the thesis of this essay that this paradox is not necessary, but Strauss is quite right in arguing that it exists. As Strauss well knows, his complaint has not jarred political analysts from their scientific moorings, and this is probably because they have imagined that analysis can be "mere." If one could "merely" analyze in a scientific way without committing oneself to a scientific view of the world, absolute commitment to the superiority of democracy would be untouched. But one cannot. Acceptance of the canons of scientific objectivity *involves* the rejection of traditional absolutism. This is just what "the crisis in Twentieth Century political theory" that Brecht speaks of is all about. Political scientists, in part at least because of the illusion that analysis can be "mere," have not seen the alternatives as scientific political science *or* democracy. Had they done so, we might expect them to behave like the physicists who remained in Germany during the Nazi period. These men, or at least a substantial portion of them, saw the alternatives as scientific advance in atomic physics *or* saving the world from destruction. Happily, they chose to drag their feet on the Nazi bomb project and thus perhaps to save the world from destruction.[10]

Scientific political scientists do not see the alternatives as scientific political science *or* democracy. If they did, scientific politics, if not dropped altogether, would surely be restricted to letters or to coded journals and would, above all, not be taught in the classroom. But Strauss and Hallowell *do* see the alternatives in this way, and essentially this is why they are so passionate in their objections to scientific political science. Both of them are philosophers enough to recognize that scientific analysis cannot be "mere" but necessarily involves a certain way of looking at the world, a way incompatible with deductive absolutism. The scientific political scientist is right in not seeing the alternatives in this way, but he is right for the wrong reasons. He seems to imagine that the scientific approach as he conceives it will not shake the foundations of democracy no matter how loudly and how frequently he tells people that their commitment to democracy is mere ideology, myth, or historically conditioned emotive preference. *"As a political scientist* I deal only with empirical facts; I exclude all value judgments," says the scientific political scientist. "This book, restricted to political analysis, declares no preferences. It states conditions." Nonsense! There is no such thing as "only dealing with empirical facts" or as "mere analysis." Any kind of analysis involves prior theoretical commitment; there are choices concealed beneath everything we say and do.

Strauss and Hallowell are right when they strike out against this naïveté, but they are wrong when they think we should abolish science and return to "classical realism." On the basis of this clash, we are told over and over again that political science and political philosophy are fundamentally incompatible. It is difficult to say which side is the more insistent. Strauss is quite explicit: " 'Scientific' political science is in fact incompatible with political philosophy."[11] We need not repeat the objections that political scientists have to political philosophy. This essay, and the literature of modern political science generally, is replete with them. I suggest that political philosophy, properly understood, and political science are no more incompatible than natural philosophy, properly understood, and physics are incompatible; in fact, they are necessary to one another. If our justification of democracy crumbles under the onslaught of critics, we shall perhaps have done service enough if we can allay this confusion.

Just as all the previous steps in our reasoning have been difficult ones, so will the remaining few as well; indeed, a final and clear statement of the justification for democracy will be the most difficult of all. In order to set the tone for the sort of solution that will be advanced, let us take a careful look at the alleged dichotomy between "problem solving in the grand tradition" and "analysis" in philosophy. "The school of analysis," as it is sometimes called, has all but demolished the conventional ways of solving problems in the grand tradition. Much of traditional cosmology, epistemology, metaphysics, and ontology (and by implication, traditional political philosophy and ethics) has fallen under its guns. The point is summed up for us by the British philosopher G. J. Warnock in the following passage (the "he" referred to is Bishop Berkeley, whose views have been under discussion):[12]

> He saw the same world that the rest of us see, but saw it from a rather different angle. It ought, of course, to be remembered that this is not all that Berkeley himself would have claimed. He did not think of himself as inventing simply a *new* way of looking at the world, but rather as expounding the *right* way, the only way in which one sees things as they really are. But this, I think, is only to say that he, like other metaphysicians, had his illusions. The builders of such imaginative systems have always been prone to claim, not that they were inventing something new, but that they were discovering something real, penetrating the disguises of Reality. But such claims are fatal as well as unfounded. For it was precisely by making these claims, by presenting themselves as super-scientists, discoverers *par excellence,* that metaphysicians drew on their own heads the formidable bludgeon of Logical Positivism. Of course there was much misunderstanding here. It was often and justly urged that the Positivists had mistaken, or disregarded, the actual character of their adversary; but this is due in large measure to the fact that their adversary, the metaphysician, had habitually presented himself in false colours. A metaphysical system, an invented conceptual apparatus, may have many virtues, such as elegance, simplicity, originality, comprehensiveness, depth, or the power to give psychological satisfaction; but the claim that any such system is exclusively true, or uniquely faithful to Reality, is a claim which sets metaphysics on quite the wrong ground, ground from which it is liable to be destructively expelled.

How well Warnock's remarks apply by analogy to the friction between scientific political science and traditional political philosophy; and of course they should, for the dispute in the study of politics is but an instance of the general philosophical controversy. Being able to see that metaphysics is not at all the "superscience" that it is thought to be is the product of careful analysis, analysis by use of the sharp tools honed by the logical positivists. We must now shift our focus to the analytical tools themselves, for in these tools of analysis and the way of looking at the world that they imply lies the solution to our problem. Again, only by seeing what *cannot* be done can we see what *can* be done.

THE ANALYSIS OF ANALYSIS

A great deal of our discussion up to this point has been built upon the claim that solutions to intellectual problems are inadequately conceived as a search for inductive or deductive proof. We have said over and over again that we must get away from the notion that "talking sense" is restricted to one or the other of these two methods of operating. We have taken some steps toward restoring the respectability of offering recommendations that cannot be "proved" by induction or deduction, and we are not yet through with this argument. Clearly, so far as modern political science is concerned, the recognition of the superior status of induction and deduction is forced upon us by adherence to what are thought to be the canons of scientific method as developed in the natural sciences. Within this view the student of politics is to restrict himself to the formulation of empirical generalizations that are to be subjected to continuing tests and, among the more sophisticated, to models of a deductive sort that are to serve a heuristic function. Recommendation is anathema because it is a part of that class of "other things," which are typically lumped to-

gether and somewhat pejoratively referred to as "value judgments." Traditional political philosophy is classed as "phony
deduction" or, for the less critical, simply as "loaded with explicit and implicit value judgments." Of course, this is a
point well taken.

As we have repeatedly said, there is much virtue in this line
of argument, but it can be—and I think has been—extended
too far. It has been pushed to the point where we are allegedly
helpless so far as philosophical recommendation in politics is
concerned. Again, this is what Brecht's "crisis in Twentieth
Century political theory" is all about. Our point is simply
that there is a very grave mistake here, and our immediate
task is to see what it is. If one wants to be unpleasant about
this insistence on scientific method, one might refer to it as
"scientism" and thus take a cue from James Ward Smith, who
says, " . . . the best antidote to scientism is a better understanding of science itself."[13]

Let me declare flatly that the conception of science which
scientific political scientists have imposed upon themselves
is far too restrictive and will not stand scrutiny when examined
in the light of examples from the natural sciences. Part of
what we shall be doing in this section, therefore, will be to
point up certain salient features of science as practiced in the
studies and laboratories, features that by no means "fit" in
the standard inductive-deductive account of scientific method.
But we shall be doing more than this. Earlier we launched a
discussion of the logic of recommendation, presenting some
notion of what could be meant by the claim that a recommendation is binding. Moreover, we argued that the corner-
stone of sound political philosophy would be a recommendation that was both binding and general, that is, binding in
every case. An examination of science will provide us with
crucial insights into the function of recommendation; above
all, it will point the way toward the formulation of a "grand"
recommendation.

Obviously the role of scientific method in political science is a vast and complicated topic. Of necessity our discussion cannot be complete in the sense of a survey. This need not, however, deter us. There is, so far as I am aware, no better and no more complete account of modern scientific political theory than that advanced by Arnold Brecht in his recent book on the subject.[14] Few political scientists have faced the philosophical presuppositions of scientific politics in the explicit way that Brecht does.

In one sense, the whole point of Brecht's book is to tell us what can and what cannot be treated by the scientific method. The number of times that he uses phrases such as "this can be determined by science" and "this is outside the realm of scientific investigation" is too enormous to make counting worth while. I stress this aspect of his remarks because it is *not* peculiar to Brecht alone; this kind of categorization has been one of the major enterprises of modern social science. Unlike physicists, who gave up this argument centuries ago, social scientists have found it necessary to spend a good deal of time disputing what kinds of problems can and cannot be dealt with scientifically. The reasons for this are obvious, and let us not suppose that this is not a worth-while enterprise. However, this passion for excluding certain kinds of statements has led to the postulation of restrictive canons of science that are far too narrow to comprehend what practicing scientists actually do. While obviously an overstatement, the following is not without purport: physicists, concerned not with restricting their enterprise but with expanding it, have been willing to use "everything but the kitchen sink" in order to make physical reality more intelligible.

Brecht goes so far as to capitalize the words "scientific method," so that "scientific method," the loose, multifaceted phenomenon that it really is, becomes "Scientific Method," the ultimate standard of inclusion or exclusion:[15]

> To begin a book on the foundations of scientific political theory in the twentieth century with a theoretical analysis of Scientific Method [sic] is justified not only on the ground that this method has dominated

scientific work; it is advisable also for several other reasons. It provides us with a clearly defined model of scientific operations, and with unambiguous terms of reference for any basic remarks in later chapters, apt to throw them automatically into sharp relief as being either in line with or in opposition to this model.

Brecht is going to provide us with a standard that will tell us in "unambiguous terms" what science can and cannot deal with. As we shall see, Brecht does not make up this standard out of whole cloth; he is essentially summarizing the standard that social scientists hold, or at least *say* they hold. Let me say again that within limits this is a very sensible thing to do. The problem is that scientific political scientists, including Brecht, go beyond those limits. To specify procedures that maximize clarity, precision, and exactitude is sensible; but to build an impenetrable wall around them is likely to be disastrous. Let us examine Brecht's "Scientific Method," which he summarizes for us in eleven points:[16]

> In every inquiry—and that means inquiry within the social as well as the natural sciences—Scientific Method concentrates on the following "scientific actions," "scientific operations," or "steps of scientific procedure":
>
> 1. *Observation* of what can be observed, and tentative acceptance or nonacceptance of the observation as sufficiently exact.
>
> 2. *Description* of what has been observed, and tentative acceptance or nonacceptance of the description as correct and adequate.
>
> 3. *Measurement* of what can be measured; this being merely a particular type of observation and description, but one sufficiently distinct and important to merit separate listing.
>
> 4. *Acceptance* or nonacceptance (tentative) as *facts* or *reality* of the results of observation, description, and measurement.
>
> 5. *Inductive generalization* (tentative) of accepted individual facts (No. 4), offered as a "factual hypothesis."
>
> 6. *Explanation* (tentative) of accepted individual facts (No. 4), or of inductively reached factual generalizations (No. 5), in terms of relations, especially causal relations, offered as a "theoretical hypothesis."
>
> 7. *Logical deductive reasoning* from inductively reached factual generalizations (No. 5) or hypothetical explanations (No. 6), so as to make explicit what is implied by them regarding other possible observations (No. 1), or regarding previously accepted facts (No. 4),

factual generalizations (No. 5), and hypothetical explanations (No. 6).

8. *Testing* by further observations (Nos. 1–4) the tentative acceptance of observations, reports, and measurements as properly made (Nos. 1–3), and of their results as facts (No. 4), or tentative expectations as warranted (No. 7).

9. *Correcting* the tentative acceptance of observations, etc., and of their results (Nos. 1–4), of inductive generalizations (No. 5) and hypothetical explanations (No. 6), whenever they are incompatible with other explanations; or correcting the previously accepted contributions.

10. *Predicting* events or conditions to be expected as a consequence of past, present, or future events or conditions, or of any possible constellation of such, in order either

(*a*) to test factual or theoretical hypotheses (Nos. 5 and 6), this being identical with steps 7 and 8; or

(*b*) to supply a scientific contribution to the practical process of choosing between several possible alternatives of action.

11. *Nonacceptance* (elimination from acceptable propositions) of all statements not obtained or confirmed in the manner here described, especially of "a-priori" propositions, except when "immanent in Scientific Method" or offered merely as "tentative assumptions" or "working hypotheses."

There is nothing very unusual about these eleven points— any social scientist would recognize them as a description of the scientific method. Brecht's view is not unique, it is typical; and this is important for us, since we are not training our analytical guns on Brecht alone but on scientific political science in general. Is this an adequate view of science?[17] We are told that one observes the facts, describes the facts, and to the extent that it is possible measures the facts. On this basis empirical generalizations are formulated, their implications are made explicit by deduction, tentative explanations are advanced, and the consequences are subjected to further tests. Does this tell the story accurately and completely? I suggest that it does not, and I do not simply mean that the chronology is erroneous or that Brecht does not go into sufficient detail. Rather, the basic conception of science presented here is erroneous in a fundamental way.

There has been a good deal of talk in recent years by scientists and philosophers of science attempting to correct the notion that science proceeds from the particular to the general. Science has been traditionally conceived as a process of gathering masses of data and building generalizations upon it. That this is not accurate has been made clear and is perhaps best summed up in Einstein's comment:[18]

> There is no inductive method which could lead to the fundamental concepts of physics . . . in error are those theorists who believe that theory comes inductively from experience.

The contrary view is that science really moves from the general to the particular, from highly abstract theoretical postulations by a process of deduction to particular propositions that can be tested by experience. Perhaps the foremost proponent of this notion is Karl Popper,[19] who tells us that

> A scientist, whether theorist or experimenter, puts forward statements or systems of statements, and tests them step by step. In the field of the empirical sciences, more particularly, he constructs hypotheses, or systems of theories, and tests them against experience by observation and experiment. . . .
>
> The theory to be developed in the following pages stands directly opposed to all attempts to operate with the ideas of inductive logic. It might be described as the theory of *the deductive method of testing,* or as the view that a hypothesis can only be empirically *tested*—and only *after* it has been advanced.

Political science is apparently beginning to regard Popper seriously, and empirical political theory of a heuristic, deductive variety has appeared in recent years.[20] Both the inductive and the deductive accounts are revealing of certain significant aspects of science; however, neither is by any means complete, and taken as such they are likely to be seriously misleading.

Brecht's eleven points seem to comprehend both induction and deduction, but the simple combination of the two does not tell the whole story of science either. Certain of the arguments that Popper makes against the inductive account will help us to focus upon the points that we want to make. If

Popper is right that one does not and cannot test an empirical hypothesis until it is formulated, immediately the question arises "Where does the hypothesis come from?" If we look at Brecht's eleven points, the answer seems to be obvious. It is formulated by inductive inference from numerous observations. But, Popper is not at all pleased with this:[21]

> According to a widely accepted view—to be opposed in this book—the empirical sciences can be characterized by the fact that they use *"inductive methods,"* as they are called. According to this view, the logic of scientific discovery would be identical with inductive logic, *i.e.* with the logical analysis of these inductive methods.
>
> It is usual to call an inference "inductive" if it passes from *singular statements* (sometimes also called "particular" statements), such as accounts of the results of observations or experiments, to *universal statements,* such as hypotheses or theories.
>
> Now it is far from obvious, from a logical point of view, that we are justified in inferring universal statements from singular ones, no matter how numerous; for any conclusion drawn in this way may always turn out to be false: no matter how many instances of white swans we may have observed, this does not justify the conclusion that *all* swans are white.

Popper is calling attention to something very significant here. He is saying that one does not and cannot by inductive inference obtain a theory to be tested against the empirical world.[22] Something else is required: one has to "jump" from experience to a theory whose implications can be tested empirically. And make no mistake, one does not climb an inductive or deductive staircase to this theory; one "jumps"! This represents a fissure in Brecht's "Scientific Method" that a little forcing will turn into a gaping hole.

Brecht or anyone who shares his notion of "Scientific Method" will not be jolted by what we have said so far. They have heard these reservations before and have an answer prepared. What one "jumps" to, it is argued, is not a *confirmed* empirical generalization—obviously, for if it were confirmed, there would be no need to jump. It is rather a "tentative assumption" or a "working hypothesis." Brecht is careful not to exclude these logical animals from the range of scientific discourse (see his point No. 11, quoted above). Popper would likely agree with this response. He dismisses the problem of how the theoretical statements are derived as being only of psychological, not philosophical, interest. Some people think up good ones, some people do not: genius is defined in these terms.[23] I suggest that in the significant cases to describe scientific theories as "tentative assumptions" or as "working hypotheses" is a very strange way of talking, persisted in only to hold up the walls that have been built around "Scientific Method." If the physicists had been limited to using what can sensibly be called "tentative empirical hypotheses,"[24] modern physics as we now understand it simply would not be.

In some ways the point that I wish to make is a linguistic one, but it is no less important for this reason. I suggest that we typically stretch the phrase "tentative empirical hypothesis" to include statements logically very different from ordinary tentative empirical hypotheses. I suggest further that this is done, albeit unconsciously, in order to preserve the philosophical purity of "Scientific Method" in the face of some highly unorthodox methods that scientists actually employ.

Let us pursue some examples in order to clarify these remarks. Suppose that I want to fit all the books in my bookcase with plastic jackets. Because I find the prospect of counting books unduly oppressive and boring, I take a dispassionate glance at my bookcase and conclude, "There are 65 books in my bookcase." We are now entertaining a genuine tentative empirical hypothesis; it may be true or false, and the possibility of confirmation or confutation is by no means mysterious. Perhaps I have counted the books on the first shelf and multiplied by the number of shelves; thus, my tentative hypothesis will be all the more scientific. On this basis I purchase 65 plastic jackets. When I go through the process of putting the jackets on the books, I will know whether my hypothesis is confirmed or refuted. If I have too many or too few jackets, I can readily correct my hypothesis.

This represents an admittedly crude example of the way in which science proceeds according to the "tentative empirical hypothesis" account. This notion will give us no trouble if we tentatively assume that the Soviets want to conquer the world à la Hitler. We may on this basis presume that their peaceful coexistence line is not to be trusted. We may be right or wrong, our hypothesis may be true or false; but in any case our bookcase example does no damage to the logic of the situation. This is to say that many things which are called tentative empirical hypotheses *are* tentative empirical hypotheses. But let us have a look at one of the more interesting statements of modern physics: "The universe is finite." How does this statement function in physical theory? Well, one may want to reply, it is a hypothesis that has not been confirmed. Is it therefore scientifically inadmissible? No, it is a "working hypothesis," a "tentative assumption," a "tentative empirical hypothesis." Surely there is something downright absurd about including "The universe is finite" in the same category as "There are 65 books in my bookcase." A finite universe is not even fathomable, let alone testable. Who has a picture in his mind of what a finite infinity would be like? I suggest that the logical characteristics of "The universe is finite" are vastly different from a genuine tentative empirical hypothesis such as "There are 65 books in my bookcase"; *but it is no less scientific on this account.*

What are we to say of a statement of this sort? It is not unique; a good many of the important notions in physics are similarly unpicturable and thus untestable in any ordinary sense. One of the most important of these is the notion that electrons are somehow both undulate and particulate. Philosopher of science Norwood Russell Hanson says of this:[25]

> If you accept this concept of electron, having properties α, β, γ (e.g. a motion formally analogous to the translation of a wave group, collision behaviour like a classical point-mass, no precisely determinable simultaneous position and velocity), then a comprehensive and systematic explanation of electron deflection, diffraction and of a

> fundamental uncertainty in microphysical experimentation will follow as a matter of course.
>
> But why should I accept this concept of an electron; since as such it is not even conceivable? "Wave-group," "point-mass"? The entity described can be no more than an ingenious mathematical combination of physically distinct parameters.
>
> You should accept it because if you do a comprehensive and systematic explanation of these diverse and apparently incompatible microphysical phenomena will follow as a matter of course. What could be a better reason?

What is Hanson telling us here? Is he telling us that the notion of a particulate and undulate electron is proved true by deduction? Not at all. Is he telling us that this notion has been proved true by empirical test? Surely not, for it is "not even conceivable." Is he then asking us to entertain the notion as a tentative working hypothesis? He does not say, "You should entertain it"; he says, "You should *accept* it." Note this language—"You *should* accept it." Is this sort of talk scientifically acceptable? The writer is using a "value" word!

Hanson makes it quite clear that the reasoning involved here is not a species of induction or deduction:[26]

> Elementary particles are not logical fictions, or mathematically divined hypotheses spirited from nowhere, to serve as bases of deductions; nor does knowledge of elementary particles consist only in a summary description of what we learn directly through large-scale observation. What we must realize, however, is that knowledge of this portion of the world is derived by means more complex than any such philosophically easy accounts suggest.

What Hanson proposes as a way of looking at the deriving of notions such as an undulate and particulate electron or a finite universe is a process of retroduction. One observes certain phenomena in the laboratory—phenomena that are apparently disparate and contradictory, such as electrons behaving sometimes as waves and sometimes as particles—and then one searches for a notion that will cause these phenomena to cohere, to "make sense." What one comes up with is not an inductive or deductive truth, nor is it a "tentative empirical hypothesis," except in the very loosest sense of this term.[27]

> This retroductive procedure, this reasoning back from observations to formulae from which the observation statements and their explanations follow, is fundamental in modern physics. Yet it is least appreciated by philosophers, so often are they attentive to the (indispensable, but sometimes over-estimated) empirical correlations of men like Boyle, Cavendish, Ampère, Coulomb, Faraday, Tyndall, Kelvin and Boys. Philosophers sometimes regard physics as a kind of mathematical photography and its laws as formal pictures of regularities. *But the physicist often seeks not a general description of what he observes, but a general pattern of phenomena within which what he observes will appear intelligible.*

What I am trying to emphasize here is that the nature of many important physical theories is grossly misunderstood if the theoretical statements are regarded *simply* as "tentative empircal hypotheses." Is it stretching language too far to say that with respect to the examples before us the physicist is saying, "Look at the world in this way. It helps."? The physicist is presented with a certain context: " . . . electrons 'veer away' from negatively charged matter; they must therefore be like particles. But electron beams diffract like beams of light, and therefore they must be like waves too." The physicist offers a recommendation that will fit the context. "[He] *fashions* the electron concept so as to make possible inferences both to its particle and its wave behavior. . . . " A "conception so fashioned is unavoidably unpicturable" and therefore unavoidably untestable in the ordinary sense. Neither is it "tentative" in any simple way. "Indeed at this point, one could have no reason to doubt the real existence of the properties; intelligibility would demand them of these sub-atomic entities."[28] This recommendation that the electron should be looked at in this way simply *is* a good recommendation in this context.

But, it may be objected, you are pushing this too far; you *are* "stretching language." Quite so, if I were to leave what I have said unqualified. But we are not here trying to replace the "tentative empirical hypothesis" view of scientific theory with *the* proper view; rather, we are essentially trying to "loosen" the notion of scientific theory, to show that the single-valued "tentative empirical hypothesis" view is not *the* proper view. There is no doubt some sense in which the concept of the undulate-particulate electron might be treated rather like an ordinary tentative empirical hypothesis, for example, if new experiments were to call for its modification or its complete rejection. But it will never be quite like "There are 65 books in my bookcase"; nor is it like "There are mountains on the other side of the moon," which before the Soviet rocket took pictures was the classic empirical hypothesis that could not be tested.[29] To test this statement would be like standing outside the universe and seeing that it is finite. What should we be standing in?

As a matter of fact, the grand theoretical statements of physics have a variety of uses, no one of which is intrinsically more correct than another. Several writers have pointed to the fact that physical laws seem to undergo a logical evolution. They begin as straightforward empirical hypotheses (it is perhaps most helpful to think here of a classical law such as the law of inertia), and then after repeated confirmation, they graduate to the status of definitions or to being held a priori. This is in effect recognized by Brecht when in his eleven steps he sees the formulation of an empirical generalization and then the deduction of consequences from it, for in order to begin deducing it is necessary to transform the logical character of the statement in question. But this account is too simple even in the area of classical mechanics, and it is even less accurate in the realm of contemporary microphysics. Professor Hanson says of this,[30]

> These authors regard the shift in a law's logic (meaning, use) as primarily of genetic interest. They agree that at any one stage in the development of physics a law is treated in just one way, as empirical or as "functionally *a priori*": in 1687 the law of inertia was apparently nothing but an empirical extrapolation; but in 1894 it functioned

mostly in an *a priori* way But this attitude is inadequate. It derives from the belief that a law sentence can at a given time have but one type of use. But the first law sentence can express as many things named "The Law of Inertia" as there are different uses to which the sentence can be put. Now, as in 1894 and in 1687, law sentences are used sometimes to express contingent propositions, sometimes rules, recommendations, prescriptions, regulations, conventions, sometimes *a priori* propositions (where a falsifying instance is unthinkable or psychologically inconceivable) and sometimes formally analytic statements (whose denials are self contradictory). Few have appreciated the variety of uses to which law sentences can be put at any one time, indeed even in one experimental report. Consequently, they have supposed that what physicists call "The Law of Inertia" is a single discrete, isolable proposition. It is in fact a family of statements, definitions and rules, all expressible via different uses of the first law sentence. Philosophers have tendered single-valued answers to a question which differs little from "What is *the* use of rope?". Once having decided their answers, they have to deprecate other obvious and, for their points of view, awkward uses of dynamical law sentences.

The reader may fairly wonder why I am belaboring these considerations in an essay alleged to be an exercise in political philosophy. Hanson's final two sentences in the passage quoted above give us the reason in a rather precise way. Philosophers and, more important for our purposes, social scientists have seen science in a way that does not correspond to its actual operations. Social scientists, seeking with great justification to emulate natural science, have oversimplified the procedures of science and in so doing have incurred disastrous concomitant effects. If one forces scientific activity into a set of neat logical pigeonholes—statements must be factual (empirical) whether tentative or confirmed, reasoning must be either inductive or deductive—then it becomes necessary, desirable, and indeed inevitable that statements and problems which do not fit cannot be dealt with scientifically and are therefore fundamentally unresolvable in any completely rational way. Nowhere is this more clear than in Brecht's exposition. After having set up "Scientific Method" in the rigid way that we discussed above, he opens the discussion of "Scientific Value Relativism," which he so aptly calls "the seamy side of Scientific Method." " . . . Scientific Value Relativism," Brecht tells us, "is the logical implication of Scientific Method. They are merely two sides of the same thing: the positive and negative side, so to speak."[31] And how could it be otherwise if scientific method is "Scientific Method," the rigid hyperempirical procedure that Brecht says it is? If science is merely a generalized description of the way the world is—only this and nothing more—then justifications for democracy of an ultimate sort *are* scientifically untenable. It is but a short step from here to the statement "A commitment to democracy is mere preference." Not only is an ultimate commitment to democracy scientifically untenable—this alone would cause no problem—but one committed to "Scientific Method," because of the view of the world that this implies, must on principle deny the possibility of an ultimate justification for democracy or for anything else. But if, as we have tried to show, scientific method is not simply a matter of logical operations based on purely empirical assertions, the contention that "Scientific Value Relativism" is implied by "Scientific Method" begins to lose some of its force.

A large part of Professor Hanson's extremely illuminating book is devoted to an elucidation of the theory-bound character of observation. He makes it clear that two observers looking at the very same problem may, because of their respective theoretical orientations, see it in entirely different ways. He cites the astronomers Tycho Brahe and Johannes Kepler watching a sunrise. Even though they both "see the same thing," one will see the sun going around the earth, while the other will see the earth rotating.[32] This is somewhat analogous to the point that we are trying to make here. If one understands scientific method as "Scientific Method," then one will simply see the problem of justifying democracy through spectacles colored by "Scientific Method." One will simply see it as impossible or as possible only in the sense that empirical observation and inductive reasoning can tell us what most people desire or what "works" with reference to some essentially arbitrary goal.[33] More than this, one will simply see scientific political science as incompatible with political philosophy. Similarly, Strauss and Hallowell will see the two as incompatible, but for different reasons.

If, however, we consider science more carefully, we shall begin to see the "philosophical" enterprise and the "scientific" enterprise as essentially compatible. "Recommending" and "fact-stating" tend to merge in scientific endeavor, and the fundamental dichotomy that has so often been interjected between the two emerges as in many important respects artificial. Yet it has not seemed at all artificial, it has seemed utterly necessary. How can we account for this? As Professor Hanson points out, scientists writing about science, philosophers of science, and, I would add, social scientists seeking to emulate natural science have concentrated on those aspects of science which make up finished, complete systems. "They have regarded as paradigms of physical inquiry not unsettled, dynamic, research sciences like microphysics, but finished systems, planetary mechanics, optics, electromagnetism and classical thermodynamics."[34] If we look at these finished systems, it is not hard to see the characteristics of science as simple fact-stating, as involving logical operations of a deductive and inductive sort.

Hanson's point of interest is, of course, very different from ours. What he has to say, however, is extremely relevant for political science. Hanson is both a physicist and a philosopher, and his problem is to find a conception of science that will comport with the activities of modern microphysicists. He is not so much concerned, as traditional philosophers of science have been, with the working out and testing of theories as he is with their discovery. Hanson is quick to point out that the traditional fact-stating, inductive-deductive account we have discussed in terms of Brecht's "Scientific Method" is inadequate for this task. Frontier research physics is not like the finished system of classical mechanics; and what is more, classical mechanics itself did not fit this pattern when it was being discovered by Newton and others. Philosophers, however, persist in treating research sciences in accordance with the model of the complete system. This, as Hanson carefully shows, is a mistake:[35]

> "After all," [the philosophers] say, "when microphysics settles down it will be like these polished systems." Such a remark constitutes a mistake in any approach to microphysics. If this attitude is accepted, the proper activity for philosophers of physics would then appear to be either (1) to study the logic of deductive systems which carry the content of microphysics, or (2) to study the statistical methods whereby microphysical theories are built up from repetitive samplings of data.

These two kinds of activity, deduction and induction, are precisely what Brecht and other "philosophers of political science" (what we become when we tell people how to engage in political science) tell us that political science should be restricted to. However, in frontier research sciences, where we are trying to *discover* theories (political science surely qualifies), this kind of advice will not do. Hanson continues,[36]

> These two approaches may apply to "classical" disciplines [i.e., classical physics]. But these are not research sciences any longer, though they were at one time—a fact that historians and philosophers of science are in danger of forgetting. Now, however, they constitute a different kind of physics altogether. Distinctions which at present apply to them ought to be suspect when transferred to research disciplines: *indeed, these distinctions afford an artificial account even of the kinds of activities in which Kepler, Galileo, and Newton themselves were actually engaged.*

The thought models implicit in Brecht's "Scientific Method" may well apply to empirical political theory after it is established, but they are misleading as an account of what science is. Hanson argues that the great physicists are essentially natural philosophers; that is, they are seeking to understand physical reality, and in so doing they are above all making recom-

mendations about the way in which the world should be
viewed. This is not all that they are doing, for they are making
inductive inferences and arriving at deductive conclusions as
well; but this is a crucial part of the scientific enterprise.
" . . . to make philosophical recommendations about the *real*
nature of the laws of dynamics—or about how law formulae
ought to be used—is exactly what the theoretical physicist is
trained for."[37] And let us be clear that these recommendations
are not simply an esoteric way of stating inductive or deductive truths. The physicist recommends that electrons be regarded as absolutely identical. This is not something which
can be tested; it is accepted because it helps in understanding
physical reality.[38] As Hanson so often says, "What could be a
better reason?"

The process of confirming and refuting statements about
the nature of the real world does not and cannot take place in
a vacuum. One does not simply begin to gather facts, generalize on the basis of the collection, and deduce from the generalization. The facts do not leap out at us—we must choose
to view the "blooming, buzzing confusion" in this way or that
way. The process of choosing carefully, of accepting this way
of looking and rejecting that way, is part of philosophy. In an
area such as microphysics the process of choosing and the
process of fact-stating and hypothesis-testing are obviously intertwined. In other areas the merger may be less obvious, but
the processes are no less intertwined. Choosing, recommending, hypothesizing, fact-stating, and deducing are all parts of
the scientific enterprise, and we do ourselves great disservice
by concentrating on only part of the process. The philosophical aspect of science is by no means a mere preliminary;
it is a crucial part of the whole enterprise. Indeed, methods of
scientific proof themselves do not arise *in vacuo;* they are the
result of a careful choice that is essentially philosophical.

We can draw two lessons from these comments on the nature of science. In the first instance, we should be somewhat
more hesitant about accepting the pronouncement that po-

litical philosophy and scientific political science are fundamentally incompatible. The process of choosing one empirical
political theory over another is essentially a matter of philosophy. We do not decide in favor of systems theory over a
balance-of-power concept in international politics on the basis
of proof, either inductive or deductive. In this sense, political
philosophy and political science work together like natural
philosophy and physics. Advances in scientific political science
will surely be based on recommending a new way of looking
at political phenomena, not merely on gathering new data.
For present purposes, the second lesson is far and away the
more important. If, as we have seen, recommendation has its
place in science—and a very important place at that—we have
no reason to dismiss it out of hand from political investigation.
To be sure, there is a great difference between recommending
what should be done in political science and recommending
what should be done in politics, but "Scientific Method" is
not the great standard of inclusion and exclusion that it has
been presumed. It is no adequate solution to lump together
all "ought" statements in the same category and to treat them
as equally specious on the grounds that they cannot be resolved
by appeal to "Scientific Method." It may be that "We ought
to adopt democracy" is on some occasions equivalent to
"Democracy, hurrah!," but it does not follow that it must always be this way—that there is no rational justification for
making the statement. Nor does it follow that the only justification is one based on inductive proof.

We have said as much as needs to be said in the present
context on our first point, namely, the validity of viewing
scientific method as "Scientific Method" and the alleged incompatibility between recommending and science. I suggested
earlier that an examination of science will give us the necessary insight for the formulation of a grand recommendation
in politics. We are now ready to take up this problem. There
are many obvious differences between science and politics,
but there are some important similarities. Above all, they are

both human activities, and in a certain sense they are both concerned with making decisions. Science can be viewed as our
way of making decisions about the way the world is; politics,
as our way of making group decisions about what the group
will do. I am not offering a definition of either science or politics here. I am instead suggesting or, if you will, recommending that we look at science and politics in this perspective, because it will help in understanding the argument that I shall
pursue.

Let us view science broadly, as a human activity that has as
its object the understanding of the way the world is, what the
facts are, or what is the case. We are not limiting ourselves to
the natural sciences or to any specialized set of academic disciplines; rather, we are treating science as the activity involved
in obtaining empirical knowledge of any sort whatsoever.
Science, considered broadly, is the process of coming to understand the way things are. The history of science so regarded
may justly be seen as an extended series of human decisions to
the effect that things are this way or that way. Many of the
decisions, if not most or all of them, have changed over time,
so that what was once a reasonable, justifiable decision is no
longer so. The history of science is a record of men changing
their minds. The question we must ask is this: What is involved in coming to understand the way things are? Or, what
must men do if they are to engage in the activity called
science? To express it yet another way, if we are to tell a man
to go out and understand the way things are, what do we tell
him to do?

We shall be dealing here with two very important and two
very closely related questions, namely, what *must* men do if
they are to engage in science and how is this "must" to be
justified? I shall argue that there are "musts" in science and
that these "musts" can be justified, in so far as justification is
possible, because in the final analysis they constitute a general and binding recommendation. My first contention, that
there are "musts" in science, is by no means obvious and not

everyone will be ready to assent to it. Some have argued that science is an essentially arbitrary procedure and that we have no reason to suppose that it is a better way of understanding the way the world is than going into a closet with a crystal ball. Our attachment to science, it is argued, is simply a culture-bound preference. Other cultures, and in the past our own culture, are not committed to it in the way that we are. There is, of course, a very great difference between saying that scientific procedure is essentially arbitrary and saying that other cultures prefer something else. The latter is hardly good evidence for the former. What really causes the difficulty here—what gives credence to the view that science is arbitrary—is that recurrent influence, the equating of justification with proof. It is surely a valid observation that science cannot be "proved true," but it does not therefore follow that science is arbitrary.

How are we to isolate the "musts" of science? The physicist J. Robert Oppenheimer, who presumably knows something about science, has pointed out that physics is learned by apprenticeship.[39] This observation can, I think, give us a valuable clue. What part of that which the master passes along to the apprentice can be regarded as fundamental—lessons which the apprentice cannot ignore if he is to become a scientist? Or are there such fundamentals at all? This is still a fair question. Note that Oppenheimer's use of the word "apprenticeship" clearly implies that something more is involved than the passing along of factual information. Apprenticeship involves instruction as to *how* something should be done, not only a recounting of what has been done. Much more is involved here than learning the proper way to roll balls down inclined planes or the proper way to correlate the results of interviews, although the development of these skills is involved in the mastery of certain sciences. What I am suggesting here is that essentially the teaching of science—this apprenticeship relation—consists in making certain philosophical recommendations as to how one is to proceed scientifically.

It is significant that the recommendations are not likely to be explicitly formulated but are more apt to be implicit in questions asked and objections advanced.[40] This characteristic is significant because the crucial recommendations are the obverse side of the recognition of the limitations of human endeavor with respect to understanding the way the world is.

A lucid way of stating the point we want to make here is as follows: one must make certain theoretical commitments if he is to proceed with science at all. To put it another way, one must make certain categorical decisions—that is, unqualified commitments—if engaging in science is to make any sense. These are "musts" of science, and the interesting question for us is what is involved in justifying them. Isolating all the "musts" of science is a task of monumental proportions that I shall not pretend to complete here. It is, however, quite possible to state some of them and thus to indicate the character of the problem.

Let us make no mistake, there are many principles to which scientists adhere that do not qualify as "musts." Some of these principles could conceivably be dispensed with, and the whole edifice of science would not crumble as a consequence. However, the rejection of certain other principles would amount to devastation of our entire concept of science. These indispensables are the "musts" that we are interested in. Let us consider some examples.

Scientists talk a good deal about the principle of parsimony. If one is confronted with two theoretical accounts, both of which explain the data in question, it is said that the simpler, more economical account should be adopted. This recommendation does not seem to qualify as a genuine "must." Surely it is a mistake to say that if one is to proceed scientifically one *must* adopt the more economical theory.[41] Undoubtedly there are good reasons for employing the simplest account possible, but science will not topple if this is not done in every case. The principle of parsimony indicates the kind of choice to be made between alternatives that are both "scientific." The genuine "musts" are thus to be found at a more fundamental level.

Consider then two principles of a very fundamental kind that are classic statements in the philosophy of science. Charles Sanders Peirce argued that science is impossible unless it is assumed that there are occurrences independent of human observation of them. One must, according to Bertrand Russell, grant that there are separable causal lines if science is to make sense. These principles are such that, assuming they are correct, science would collapse upon their serious rejection. It is important to notice here that neither Russell nor Peirce is presenting us with a report of what scientists *say* they do. What both are saying is that this is what scientists in fact *do* when they are functioning as scientists. Peirce would not be disturbed by a scientist who professed solipsism, nor would Russell be alarmed if it could be demonstrated that he was saying something that no scientist had ever thought of. What both are saying is that there are "musts" implicit in the conduct of science. The scientist acts upon them whether or not it has occurred to him that he is doing so.[42] It should be noted that natural scientists have no special claim to these premises; they are equally the property of anyone who professes empirical knowledge of anything whatsoever.

How can we be sure that Peirce or Russell is right? How can we know that there are "musts" in science? Perhaps the best way of getting at the answers to these questions is to state the case *against* the necessity of categorical commitments in science as forcefully as we can. It can, as we have suggested, be argued that there is nothing imperative about the use of science as a method of empirical inquiry. Upon investigation it is clear that science is essentially arbitrary. It must be taken on faith, "animal faith" as George Santayana once put it. This is the argument we often encounter in sermons on Sunday morning. Science, we are told, does not damage the theological edifice because it, too, is ultimately a matter of faith. But let us, as I suggest, state the case more forcefully. The mere fact that we can use the noun "science" does not ensure that science is in any sense a definite object. Science, as we ourselves have testified earlier, is in reality an amorphous complex of loosely connected activities that are in turn loosely described as "scientific." If, it might be argued, one wants to say what is involved in science, two alternatives are open:[43]

> (i) You may at any given time describe the more predominant traits shared by the hodgepodge of activities called "scientific"; these descriptions will vary from time to time; and such uniformities as you discover are no more nor less than the uniformities which show up in these descriptions. There is nothing in all this which will allow you to insist that there is any one thing you *must* do in order to engage in science.
>
> (ii) You may legislate by fiat either that what you have found common, or that something you personally choose to do, is to be taken as the defining trait (or traits) of science. In such case, of course, anyone must do that kind of thing in order to engage in what you call "science"; but the "must" is now reduced to a matter of definition. Obviously, for example, if you define "science" as (in part) a method of approach which ignores moral considerations in choosing between alternative hypotheses [à la Brecht], then you must (in part) ignore moral considerations in choosing between alternative hypotheses if you are engaging in science; but the "must" here merely reveals that you are so defining the word "science."

We have two problems before us. The first problem is whether there are "musts" in science at all, and the second is how these "musts" can be justified. I wish now to suggest that these two problems tend upon examination to merge into one. Stating the "musts" of science involves justifying them and justifying science itself. How can we say they are "musts" unless we can justify their necessity? Look carefully at the argument set forth above, which holds that science is essentially arbitrary and not a matter of "musts" at all. We are being told that science is essentially arbitrary because it is impossible to *prove* that there is anything necessary about the method of approaching empirical reality which we call science. We return again to our fundamental theme. We are told that an inductive inference from observed common practices by scientists does not allow us to conclude that these practices are essential. We might always be able to find the counter instance of someone who investigated reality and employed none of these practices. In order to escape this difficulty, we must define science in a certain way, and only in this way we are able to use the word "must." But this "must" has no genuine force, for we have merely posited it, and our demonstration of a *particular* "must" by deduction from it would therefore not be binding with respect to the real world.

All this is but a way of saying what has often been said, that one cannot *prove* the validity of the rules of scientific procedure by the rules of scientific procedure. One cannot prove the validity of deduction and induction by deduction and induction. We are inclined to say that this is a matter of no great import for the scientist *qua* scientist. His concern is to convince other scientists who share a commitment to these rules of procedure that an empirical statement is established. He is not called upon in every case to validate scientific method, for scientists agree upon it already. But this is to say nothing about the philosophical problem involved, which is "Why these rules of procedure and not some others?"[44]

Perhaps no other situation makes the contention that it is a mistake to equate justification with proof so clear as this one. What could be more absurd than to say that there are no reasons for choosing scientific procedure over other procedures when we are interested in discovering the nature of empirical reality? But if it is clear that the validity of these procedures cannot be proved, and that justifying is the same thing as proving, what other conclusion are we to come to? Few philosophers have been content to leave the problem at this, and the history of philosophy is replete with attempts to assimilate induction into deduction or to prove induction by induction.[45] It is no secret that all these attempts have failed—later philosophers have been more than willing to show the inadequacy of the alleged proof. This is but additional testimony to the correctness of the view that the validity of scientific procedures cannot be *proved* by scientific procedures. To take the equating of justification and proof seriously means that, if as political scientists we want to find out why the British have a two-party system, there is nothing to choose between sitting atop the Tower of London waiting for a mystical vision, examining the meter in Tennyson's *Idylls of the King*, and studying the formation of political alliances in Parliament before 1832. Obviously, there *is* a rational choice to be made, and if our methods of philosophizing lead us to conclude that there is not, we had better recognize that there is something wrong with our methods of philosophizing. For just this reason, we contend that justification is not always identical with proof. We can either continue to demand proof and ignore the fact that our demand has not been met—continuing, thus, to behave as if scientific procedures have been proved valid, when in fact they have not; or we can face the fact that a demand for proof is out of place here and ask instead the proper question: How are scientific procedures to be rationally justified?

People who treat science as essentially arbitrary do not understand what they are looking at. They miss certain crucial aspects of scientific activity. Perhaps we can best see the point here by examining something that actually fits the description which is offered for science. What we are being told is that science is a human activity which may have definite rules of procedure but that these rules of procedure are essentially arbitrary. Many people engage in this activity, and there seems to be a certain common ground for all of them. This common ground—these common rules of procedure—can be dealt with in two ways: discover what the common rules actually are by empirical investigation or posit a set of rules as defining the activity. In either of these ways it is possible to say what science is, but neither of them gives us any reason to suppose that it *must* be this way. This seems to me a perfectly adequate way of dealing with a popular game; thus it is no accident that positivist philosophers have spent a great deal of time talking about the rules of games. The game analogy has as a matter of fact been frequently used. Examples and analogies in modern analytical philosophy drawn from chess alone must number in the thousands.

Personally, I prefer poker to chess—which may go to prove that I am more political scientist than philosopher after all. In any case poker will do very nicely as illustration for the points that need to be made. Suppose that we were to ask, "What are the 'musts' of poker?" First of all, it should have to be noted that poker has an extraordinary number of variations. Every table of poker players to some extent makes up its own rules; indeed, the initial stage of almost any poker game is a solemn contract concerning a betting limit, a limit on the number of raises, whether or not "a circle straight is any good in this game," etc. I remember once reading a Mutt and Jeff cartoon in which the two were engaged in a poker game. Jeff, who showed four kings, was ready to take the pot when Mutt showed his hand, four clubs and a spade, which Mutt said was called a "razz-goo" and beat anything. Later when Jeff tried to take a pot on four clubs and spade, he was informed that the second time such a hand appeared it was called a "razz-razz" and didn't beat anything. We can certainly question the propriety of this, but only because these rules were not set down beforehand. Poker *is* essentially arbitrary—it is a game and nothing more. In answer to a question about the "musts" of poker, we can only seek to establish certain common practices by empirical investigation, or we can prescriptively define poker in terms of certain procedures. But it would make no sense to talk of the "ultimate musts" of poker. This is simply because it is arbitrary—we can play or not play, play stud or draw, or even play with dice and call it poker if we want to—and it makes no difference.[46]

But science is not a mere game; it is not arbitrary in this sense, and this makes all the difference. Considering science through the analogy of a game may be helpful in some respects, but if we take the comparison too seriously, we shall miss its most important features. As Smith puts it,[47]

> The reason we do not call science a game is that it is a complex of activities engaged in with a significant purpose. We are willing to accept arbitrary fiats as sufficient to establish basic rules only so long as what we are *doing* is arbitrary. For this reason we are willing to concede that the basic rules of bridge or chess [or poker] are arbitrary fiats. No one could deny for a moment that when we engage in science we do as a matter of fact constantly lay down arbitrary fiats; but in this case we are not satisfied. In a game, the rules are laid down; you may play it or not as you choose; it makes no important difference one way or the other. In science what is laid down is a purpose—sometimes vague, sometimes relatively clear. We want to find out all we can about something, or we want to achieve control of a situation by accurate prediction. The purpose being laid down, the whole point of science is to develop a set of rules which will be dependable. Laying down the rules is not something which is done "outside" the "game"; it is not a *fait accompli* before we start to play. We do not read up the rule books and then sit down to play. Playing here *is* an attempt to examine and re-examine the rules to find out which we can and which we cannot avoid.

The aim of science is to find out the way the world is. This is not a metaphysical statement. I do not mean it in any Aristotelian teleological sense. I simply mean that men do as a matter of fact try to find out the way things are, and this activity is what we are talking about when we use the term "science." It is of the utmost importance that we recognize that men begin and continue to engage in this activity against a background of extraordinary ignorance. It is in this context that the general and binding recommendation that is the consummate "must" of science functions. The ignorant, finite, limited man seeks to understand the world. "How should he do it?"—that is the question. We have said a good deal about what man *cannot* do with respect to his intellectual problems. We have seen the limited character of deductive inference—that it is analytic and cannot therefore inform us about the real world save in a heuristic way. Furthermore, we have seen that inductive inference cannot establish certitude. We have seen how these limitations lead us to conclude that scientific rules of procedure cannot be *proved* valid and that it therefore seems that they are arbitrary. What we must now see is that in the very recognition of these limitations lies the justification of scientific procedure. These limitations are simply ways of detailing man's inadequacy with respect to knowing about the world. By seeing these limitations—by seeing what *cannot* be done—we are able, by simply shifting our focus, to see what *can* be done (or better, what *must* be done) if we are to approach intellectual problems rationally. If, as I have suggested, the important question is "How should man operate given this purpose and these limitations?," the answer cannot be an empirical statement that is *proved* to be true. It must be a recommendation that is binding in the context.

I wish now to quote what is perhaps as profound a paragraph as has ever been written:[48]

> Upon this first, and in one sense this sole, rule of reason, that in order to learn you must desire to learn, and in so desiring not be satisfied with what you already incline to think, there follows one corollary which itself deserves to be inscribed upon every wall of the city of philosophy:
> Do not block the way of inquiry.

Charles Sanders Peirce, to whose remarks I here call attention, has been called by many the greatest of American philosophers. Peirce saw clearly, as few others have, that the very recognition of human intellectual limitations in itself supplies the maxim which should govern behavior. Like all really profound insights, what Peirce tells us here is in some ways very simple. Very few people would quarrel with the observation that with respect to matters of fact we can never be absolutely certain. But perhaps even fewer clearly see that this same statement also tells what to do. What Peirce tells us is that, if we are engaged in trying to understand how things are, it is never rational to block the way of inquiry. We are never justified in behaving as if a question of fact has been absolutely and finally settled, for new evidence might always be forthcoming. We shall need to explore very carefully the implications of Peirce's maxim, for it is very easy to misunderstand; however, let me first call explicit attention to the logical character of what Peirce tells us. "Do not block the way of inquiry"—this is the crucial statement. Note, please, that this is neither a statement of empirical fact nor an analytic truth. Thus, it is utterly inappropriate to ask that it be *proved* true or false. It is cast in the imperative mood, precisely the way in which Peirce intends it. This is a recommendation: it does not say what is, it says what to do. Nowhere is the value of the analytic movement in philosophy more clear than here. Unless we recognize the distinction between statements that can be true or false—empirical statements, the logically true, and the logically false—and statements that can be neither true nor false, we shall never rise out of the hopeless intellectual morass created by the looseness of our own language. In ordinary parlance "true" and "false" are loosely used, but it is essential that we recognize the difference between saying that "Do not block the way of inquiry" is "true," and saying that "Water flows downhill" is true or that "All bachelors are unmarried" is true. On this basis we are able to see that justification is not always a matter of proof.

I suggest that the maxim "Do not block the way of inquiry" is a statement of the ultimate "must" of science. This is the essence of what the master passes on to the apprentice. This is what all genuine scientists have in common, whether their point of interest is physics, biology, or politics. It may never become explicit in the teaching of a particular science, but it is a summing up of what we call the "scientific attitude" wherever it is employed. If, as I suggest, this is an overriding "must," it must be absolutely justified and must admit of no exceptions. How can we say that it is absolutely justified? It is justified as a recommendation that fits the context we are interested in, that is, men with limited capacities seeking to understand the world. With all the intellectual vigor we can command, we must resist the temptation to cast this justification into a syllogism. To show that this recommendation follows by de-

duction from a set of premises is precisely what cannot be
done. There may perhaps be an objection to this line of argument, which should be dealt with at this point. It might be
asserted that Peirce's recommendation is in fact an ends-
means argument which might be put in the following way:
"If you desire truth, then do not block the way of inquiry."
Examination shows, however, that this account cannot be accurate, for not blocking the way of inquiry is no guarantee of
truth. Scientific procedures can, of course, produce a limitless
series of errors. Ends-means analysis breaks down with respect
to general recommendations of this sort. Peirce's categorical
argument is a way of stating within the context of investigating empirical reality a wholly general maxim that might be
phrased in a number of ways (e.g., "Be rational," "Be self-
critical," "Do not act as if you have the Truth when you cannot
be certain that you have it").

It is perhaps helpful to put the justification of Peirce's
statement in this way: we would be justified in blocking the
way of inquiry if, and only if, we were certain that we had
found the absolute truth with respect to a certain point. Since
this can never be, in so far as we seek to establish the nature of
reality, "Do not block the way of inquiry" is always justified as
a recommendation. We must now call attention to a consideration of the utmost importance. Peirce's maxim, "the principle
of fallibilism," as he called it, does not prescribe universal
skepticism. One is tempted to read it this way, but such an
interpretation is to misunderstand his intent. The principle of
fallibilism does not say that we can never know the truth, but
rather that we are never justified in behaving as if we knew it.
That is to say, we are never justified in refusing to consider the
possibility that we might be wrong. Every time a hypothesis is
verified (the weight of the evidence supports it), we are assured
that we are not *wholly wrong;* but we can never be assured
that we are *wholly right.* If it happens that we do come
up with complete truth with respect to a certain question, the
principle of fallibilism can do it no harm. A complete truth

will continue to stand, even if we continue to investigate other possibilities; but the moment we assume that it is complete truth, we cut off the ever-present possibility that we might be wrong. Peirce does not say that we cannot reliably predict that the sun will rise in the east, but he does say that we are not justified in refusing to entertain the possibility that it is the movement of the earth rather than that of the sun that brings this about.

Let us face the fact that in one sense the justification of fallibilism as the overriding "must" of science is circular. It is generally supposed that calling a piece of reasoning "circular" is the most devastating attack that can be leveled against it; but it is a mistake to suppose that all circles are vicious. What we are contending is that we are rationally obligated to behave as if we are limited with respect to knowledge of matters of fact because we *are* so limited. The examination of our own tools of analysis reveals these limitations. Knowledge of our instruments shows us at once what we can do and what we cannot do. Inductive generalization can be a very effective way of operating, and as scientists, we are wise to use it. On the basis of inductive generalizations, we can reliably predict events and can in these terms control the world around us. Engineers do it all the time. But inductive generalizations always admit of exceptions, and it is therefore never rational to refuse to recognize the possibility that an exception may come along. Understanding of the world as it really is cannot proceed if we so refuse. It must in this area come to a halt. This is blocking the way of inquiry.

Deductive inference is a very important intellectual process. We can predict events by this method, as the role of mathematics in scientific development has shown us. We can deduce with absolute certainty—the meanings we attach to the terms assure us of this. But deductive conclusions can always be wrong, because we can never be sure that our premises correspond to the world as it really is. To refuse to recognize this, to regard the premises as absolutely true, is never justifiable, simply because we have no way of knowing that they are true. Such a refusal is irrational; it blocks the way of inquiry, and to do this is to bring the process of understanding the world to a halt. Not even direct experience justifies blocking the possibility that we might be wrong. Fallibilism does not prescribe that I never say "I see the sun" because I might be dreaming or because it might really be an atomic explosion; but it does prescribe that I not refuse to entertain such possibilities.

I have used the words "rational" and "irrational" several times in the last few paragraphs. This links up with our earlier remarks with respect to the question "What does it mean to be rational?" We have been led to suppose that we are only rational when we deal in deductive systems or when we base our conclusions on empirical generalization. Any assertion of preference or any recommendation is widely held to contain an element of irrationality, if not to be wholly irrational. "You cannot *prove* it, therefore to maintain it is irrational." But what can "rationality" possibly mean if it is not rational to assent to the recommendation "Do not block the way of inquiry"? What could be more clear than that rational justification is not always a matter of proof?

There is but one further point to be made. Again we return to a former theme. We argued earlier that analysis could never be "mere" and suggested that by committing ourselves to standards of analysis we were at the same time committing ourselves to a view of the world. The maxim implied in a self-critical examination of what we are capable of doing reaches far beyond the professional pursuit of science. It provides us with a place to stand when we look at the world and our problems with respect to it. Methods of analysis are never neutral; they are only self-critical or not. Self-criticism gives us a standard of judgment with respect to dealing rationally with our problems. The problem to which we shall now turn is the choice of a political system. All the foregoing is instruction as to what is involved in making this choice a rational one.

NOTES

1 James Ward Smith, *Theme for Reason* (Princeton, N.J.: Princeton University Press, 1957), p. 137.

2 D. J. O'Conner, *John Locke* (Baltimore: Penguin Books, Inc., 1952), p. 12.

3 Cf. Smith, *op. cit.*, p. 138. (Italics in original.)

4 Ludwig Wittgenstein, *Tractatus Logico-Philosophicus* (London: Routledge & Kegan Paul Ltd., 1922), 4.112, p. 77. "The object of philosophy is the logical clarification of thoughts." ("Der Zweck der Philosophie ist die logische Klärung der Gedanken.")

5 Immanuel Kant, *Prolegomena To Any Future Metaphysics* (New York: Liberal Arts Press, 1950), p. 3.

6 Cf. Smith, *op. cit.*, pp. 137–168.

7 Cf. A. J. Ayer, *Language, Truth and Logic* (New York: Dover Publications, 1953).

8 Harold D. Lasswell, *Politics: Who Gets What, When, How* (New York: Meridian Books, Inc., 1958), p. 13. (Italics added.)

9 Leo Strauss, *What Is Political Philosophy? and Other Studies* (New York: The Free Press of Glencoe, Inc., 1959), p. 222.

10 See Robert Jungk, *Brighter Than A Thousand Suns* (New York: Harcourt, Brace & World, Inc., 1958).

11 Strauss, *op. cit.*, p. 14.

12 G. J. Warnock, "Analysis and Imagination," final essay in A. J. Ayer et al., *The Revolution in Philosophy* (London: Macmillan & Co., Ltd., 1956), pp. 122–123. Quoted in Smith, *op. cit.*, pp. 139–140. (Italics in original.)

13 Smith, *op. cit.*, p. 178.

14 Arnold Brecht, *Political Theory: The Foundations of Twentieth Century Political Thought* (Princeton, N.J.: Princeton University Press, 1959).

15 *Ibid.*, pp. 27–28. It is only fair to note that Brecht does not leave these remarks unqualified, *but* his qualifications are extraneous to the point we are making. He wants to concede that childhood remembrances, mystical visions, etc., may be true even though science cannot verify them (see pp. 113–116 of his book). We are concerned not with what may in some mystical sense be "really true" but with what can be neither true ncr false.

16 *Ibid.*, pp. 28–29. (Italics in original.)

17 Let us be clear that Brecht expands each of these points in his discussion. Nothing that he says, however, vitiates the points that we shall make against it.

18 Albert Einstein, *The Method of Theoretical Physics* (New York: Oxford University Press, 1933). Quoted in Norwood Russell Hanson, *Patterns of Discovery: An Inquiry into the Conceptual Foundations of Science* (New York: Cambridge University Press, 1959), p. 119.

[19] From Karl R. Popper, *The Logic of Scientific Discovery.* © 1959 by Karl Popper. (New York: Basic Books, Inc., Publishers), pp. 27–30. (This is a translation of the famed *Logik der Forschung* of 1934. Italics in original.)

[20] For example, Anthony Downs, *An Economic Theory of Democracy* (New York: Harper & Brothers, 1957); and Morton Kaplan, *System and Process in International Politics* (New York: John Wiley & Sons, Inc., 1957).

[21] Popper, *op. cit.,* p. 27. (Italics in original.)

[22] See Popper's remarks, *ibid.,* pp. 28–32.

[23] " . . . my view of the matter, for what it is worth, is that there is no such thing as a logical method of having new ideas, or a logical reconstruction of this process. My view may be expressed by saying that every discovery contains 'an irrational element,' or 'a creative intuition,' in Bergson's sense." *Ibid.* See also Brecht, *op. cit.,* pp. 30–31.

[24] Note here that I have, in order to make the contention more precise, added the word "empirical" to Brecht's language. So far as I can see, however, this adds nothing to his meaning. Whenever he discusses these "tentative assumptions" or "working hypotheses," he seems always to be talking about something which might *really* be the case, i.e., about a "fact" which cannot be or has not been verified. See Brecht, *op. cit.,* pp. 456–477.

[25] Hanson, *op. cit.,* pp. 108–109. For a good discussion of the electron as wave and particle, see Sir Harrie Massey, F.R.S., *The New Age in Physics* (New York: Harper & Brothers, 1960), pp. 43–66.

[26] Hanson, *op. cit.,* pp. 124–125.

[27] *Ibid.,* p. 109. (Italics added.)

[28] *Ibid.,* p. 123. (Italics added.)

[29] See Ayer, *op. cit.,* p. 36.

[30] Hanson, *op. cit.,* p. 98. (Italics in original.) For expansion of these remarks, *ibid.,* pp. 99–118.

[31] Brecht, *op. cit.,* p. 118.

[32] Hanson, *op. cit.,* pp. 4–30.

[33] Note remarks in Brecht, *op. cit.,* pp. 387–416.

[34] Hanson, *op. cit.,* p. 1.

[35] *Ibid.*

[36] *Ibid.* (Italics added.)

[37] *Ibid.,* pp. 2, 88, 107, 113, 119. (Italics in original.)

[38] *Ibid.,* pp. 129, 133–134.

[39] J. Robert Oppenheimer, *Science and the Common Understanding* (New York: Simon and Schuster, Inc., 1954).

[40] Cf. Smith, *op. cit.,* p. 178.

[41] Cf. *ibid.,* p. 179.

[42] Cf. *ibid.*

43 *Ibid.*, pp. 180–181. (Italics in original.) This does not represent Smith's own view but is part of his statement of the alternative view.

44 Cf. Richard Bevan Braithwaite, *Scientific Explanation* (New York: Cambridge University Press, 1953), pp. 262–264.

45 Cf. Brecht, *op. cit.*, pp. 55–63, 113–116.

46 Cf. Smith, *op. cit.*, pp. 181–182.

47 *Ibid.* (Italics in original.)

48 Charles Sanders Peirce, "The Scientific Attitude and Fallibilism" in Justus Buchler (ed.), *Philosophical Writings of Peirce* (New York: Dover Publications, 1955), p. 54.

8

DEMOCRACY IN PRINCIPLE

"There are crimes of passion and crimes of logic. The boundary between them is not clearly defined. But the Penal Code makes the convenient distinction of premeditation. We are living in the era of premeditation and the perfect crime. Our criminals are no longer helpless children who could plead love as their excuse. On the contrary, they are adults and they have a perfect alibi: philosophy, which can be used for any purpose—even for transforming murderers into judges."[1] The problems of political philosophy are in the modern era, perhaps as never before, matters of life and death. Political philosophy is used as a tool for the justification of murder and oppression on a grand scale.

These may perhaps seem strange words to inject into the argument that has gone before. We have tried to analyze in a highly technical way, for no other reason than that this is a highly technical problem. But in being analytical and technical, we must not lose sight of the fact that we are dealing, however inadequately, with a profoundly human problem. It is a problem of the mind, but it is also a problem of the body. If political philosophy has been used to "transform murderers into judges," it is the obligation of the political philosopher to put these reasonings to the test of rationality. If they make sense, that is one thing; but if they do not, we must see clearly why they do not. If an alternative that puts a premium on human life and free expression does make sense, we must see clearly why it does. This is what political philosophy is for.

To see these problems clearly is to see them as highly technical questions. We have had all the vague, emotive outbursts that we need in political philosophy. If close analysis will help to straighten out our thinking, then let us have it. As Sir Isaiah

Berlin once remarked, " . . . philosophical concepts nurtured in the stillness of a professor's study could destroy a civilization . . . if professors can truly wield this fatal power, may it not be that other professors, and they alone, can disarm them?"[2] Despite our close analysis, however, we dare not lose sight of the background of human misery and happiness against which our analysis is conducted.

What we are talking about is perhaps the most important problem that faces modern man. While we may operate in a rarified atmosphere, inhabited by excursus on the empirical hypothesis and the analyticity of deductive inference, at root the problem is one for men in all walks of life. We are talking about ultimate political choice, between open society and closed society, between democracy and totalitarianism. One can approach this problem in many different ways. We have moved toward it by means of a logical analysis of the notion of rational justification, because this seems to me the most fruitful way. We have thus taken logical positivism as our philosophical point of departure; and if one searches for a term that will describe the line we have taken, perhaps "postpositivist" is as good as any. Our situation is typically and peculiarly modern: we are not willing to accept traditional natural-law deductive absolutism, nor are we satisfied with relativism. This major dilemma of twentieth-century political thought is what we are striving to deal with. It is a dilemma that forces itself not only upon Americans and Englishmen of an analytical bent but on continental Europeans of existentialist inclinations as well. In a certain sense, logical positivism and existentialism have arisen to confront the same problem. In more ways than adherents of both positions would like to admit, they are similar. They both follow in the wake of the problem created by modern science, the problem of limited and finite man faced with an inscrutable universe. The positivists have striven to point out and delimit the narrow area in which these finite men can operate, and thus they have tried to limit us to talking empirical hypotheses and tautologies. What is left is said to be a realm of irrationality, a realm of emotion. The existentialists, feeling the profound inadequacy of this view, have asked us to take a leap of faith into this irrational realm.[3] It is either this or, as some have contended, nothingness.

But is this move away from the empirical hypothesis and the tautology really irrational? From our "postpositivist" position, we have said "no" and have, I think, shown why. It strikes me that there is a "postexistentialist" approach to this problem as well, one that I find insufficient for reasons of linguistic imprecision and therefore, I can presume, of intellectual imprecision. Nevertheless, there is insight here. The remarkable Albert Camus seeks a rational ground for upholding the illegitimacy of murder, striking out in this way against Nazi and Communist totalitarianism. What is instructive here is the place from which Camus begins. "The important thing," he tells us, " . . . is not . . . to go to the root of things, but, the world being what it is, to know how to live in it."[4] Sound philosophizing requires that we stop addressing ourselves to fundamentally unanswerable questions such as "What is *the* purpose of life?"; "What is *the* nature of man?"; "What is *the* meaning of the universe?"; and that we begin to face the question with which we can deal—which, as it happens, is also the really important question. The question is simply this: "The human situation being what it is, what is it rational to do?" We are here; now what do we do? We have a context; what is the best recommendation in this context? By way of introduction we gave an answer to the problem with respect to science; but our main problem involves what we do in politics.

Quite clearly, the first thing we must do in answering this question is to make specific the important aspects of the political context. It is all important that we be quite clear about the point from which we start. We begin with a context, with a situation. As a minimum, we must have a group of men and someone who is interested in setting up a procedure to make decisions for the group. This is not a premise which has to be justified or proved, it is simply a minimal statement of the situation that brings political philosophy into being. If there were no groups of men and if there were no question of making decisions for the group, there would be no political philosophy.

It is important that we stress this starting place, that we see the logical character of this statement of context. As soon as we begin to say that "men *by nature* live in groups" or that "men *ought* to live in groups," we put ourselves in an indefensible position. The "truth" of these propositions, in so far as they are propositions, is something—as Peirce and others have shown—that we cannot know for certain. Thus, a political philosophy that starts from these "truths" or similar ones is faulty from the beginning. I do not, I presume, need to point out that a great deal of the history of political philosophy is marked by first premises of this sort. "Man is by nature a political animal" and "Men are motivated by a desire to preserve their own lives" begin political philosophies equally on the wrong foot. To talk "first premises" is to talk in terms of "proof," and this is precisely what must be avoided. We start therefore not with fundamental axioms but with a context.

How much needs to be said about this context? Its dimensions are vast and its variables myriad. The whole corpus of political science is more or less relevant to describing it completely. For present purposes we need, however, only point up certain significant features. As indicated, men in groups and decisions taken for the group are our basic points of interest. It would, I think, be a mistake to say much more about the men involved—at this point in our analysis at any rate. Clearly, when one seeks to install a certain political system among a particular group of men in the real world, the sort of men who make up the group is an extremely important factor. Their social and religious habits, their educational level, their experience with government, and their economic situation are all highly relevant to the problem of constructing an institutional arrangement. But to introduce these considerations is unnecessarily to encumber philosophical investigation, for these are essentially empirical matters which we should have to deal with not by philosophical speculation but by observation. Different men will require different institutional arrangements, but matters of principle are relevant to all men; and for the moment we are talking about matters of principle.

More, however, needs to be said about the character of political decisions—or to be more precise, "governmental" decisions. Here I think David Easton's definition of politics is helpful. Easton suggests that the political process can be described as "the authoritative allocation of values for a society."[5] I do not suggest nor, I think, does Easton, that this is *the* definition of politics, but merely that it is helpful to look at our context in this way. The central concern of this essay may be fairly described as the rational choice of a decision-making procedure[6] that will authoritatively allocate values for a society. We need not trouble ourselves with the use of the word "authoritative," which is simply another way of saying "governmental." What does need attention is the notion of allocating values. At core, any governmental decision on public policy denies certain things to some people and makes them accessible to others.[7] In this sense a government authoritatively allocates values for a society, not all values to be sure, but an important portion of them. Unless one is ready to accept a most rigid determinism, the allocation of values inevitably involves choice among alternatives. It is important that we look with some care at the character of choice in this context.

Whoever does the choosing of one alternative over others will presumably be attempting to effect a certain end by this choice. Decisions are not made, nor are policies inaugurated, just for the sake of making decisions or inaugurating policies, although it is not inconceivable that this should happen. Choosing a policy thus involves, at least implicitly, a prediction as to a matter of fact. This is not to say that decision makers are always quite sure what will happen as a consequence of making a certain decision. It is to the everlasting

credit of democratic decision makers especially that they sometimes experiment with legislation. But it is fair to say that some
prediction, however loose, is a part of the adoption of a governmental decision. That there is uncertainty here is precisely
what we need to recognize. Moreover, this uncertainty is compounded by the possibility—indeed the very great likelihood
—that even if immediate effects can be predicted with high
accuracy, long-term effects, or the effect of this decision in
the context of all decisions, will be even more unpredict-
able.

Of course, this is not all that is involved in such decision
making. We must also introduce the notion of value. Even if
effects could be predicted with absolute accuracy, which is
patently not the case, people can and will differ over the de-
sirability of these effects. Questions of value may arise anywhere along the line, with respect to short, intermediate, or
long-range effects. Moral philosophers such as C. L. Stevenson
have found it helpful to approach an analysis of ethics by concentrating on what is involved in ethical argument. In this
connection Stevenson[8] notes,

> When ethical issues become controversial, they involve disagree-
> ment that is of a *dual* nature. There is almost inevitably disagreement
> in belief, which requires detailed, sensitive attention; but there is also
> disagreement in attitude.

It is, of course, obvious that we can regard political choices as
matters of controversy and can thus make our point in Stevenson's language. There can be differences with respect to belief
(i.e., with respect to matters of fact); and even if the questions
of fact can be resolved, differences in attitude (i.e., preference)
may remain.

Man's situation in politics is but an aspect of his situation
in the world generally. The overriding characteri   of this
situation is one of ignorance, of limited intellectua capacity.
Socrates was right when he suggested that the essence of wisdom was the recognition of our intellectual limitations. The

recognition of these limitations *is* the foundation of sound philosophizing. The human problem with respect to politics is not unlike the human problem with respect to science. Both arise against a background of ignorance and incapacity, and both are to be solved by recognizing these limitations. Peirce could posit a general recommendation as the overriding "must" of science, and we must likewise find a general recommendation that will serve as the overriding "must" of politics.

If the political context is as we describe it—involved with predictions as to matters of fact that cannot be resolved with certitude, compounded by value preferences which similarly cannot be resolved—our problem of the rational choice of a decision-making procedure begins to show itself as soluble. It is soluble if we look for a recommendation that can be justified in context, not for a theorem that can be proved by demonstration.

As we approach this problem, we should do well to again call to mind the directive we examined earlier; namely, only by seeing what *cannot* be done we see what *can* be done. Our introductory question is thus "What cannot be done in political philosophy?" Let me answer this at first categorically and then undertake a justification for my answer. My answer is this: political philosophy cannot demonstrate in any ultimate sense that rule by one or by a few is the ideally best form of government. I do not need to say that a good many political philosophers have attempted precisely this; but they have always failed and, I suggest, always will fail. Let us be careful that we do not say too much here. I do not intend to suggest that it is never reasonable for one man or for a few men to make decisions for a society in the real world. It is, of course, quite a reasonable proposal in a complex nation such as the United States, and it may be equally reasonable in politically under-developed societies. What I do intend to say is that it is never reasonable at the level of ultimate principle or, if you will, at the "ideal" level. One may quite plausibly argue that foreign policy decisions in the United States need to be taken by one man or by a small group of men—given certain goals, the necessity of speedy action, etc.; in short, *as a matter of practicability*. But as a matter of ultimate principle, and this is where political philosophers ordinarily operate, it is never reasonable.

Let us see what kinds of arguments the political philosopher could advance in support of elite rule as a matter of ultimate principle. We deal here both with conceivable arguments and with arguments that as a matter of historical fact have been advanced. Professor Leslie Lipson presents the major arguments diagrammatically:[9]

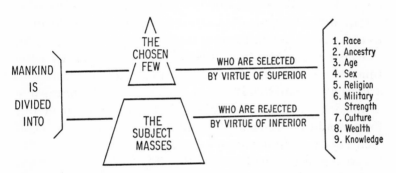

We can, I think, dismiss the first eight arguments simply as quite untenable. Surely, it is possible to divide mankind in terms of age, ancestry, race, etc. These are empirical matters: it is quite possible to tell whether a man is white or black, rich or poor, over sixty or under sixty. However, it is quite impossible to show that men differentiated by these criteria *ought* to rule. The logical illegitimacy here should be clear, and in any case we have discussed it in detail earlier. It is consummately obvious that one cannot demonstrate that white men are alone capable of making wise decisions for societies, and I presume we need say no more.

Lipson's ninth point, the criterion of knowledge, is in a different category. It is at once the most interesting, most intricate, and, so far as the contemporary political situation is concerned, the most important argument for elite rule. In one sense it is plausible; that is, if we take "knowledge" to mean "experience" or "qualification for office." In this limited sense we may want to choose leaders in terms of their knowledge and experience, but this is by no means a binding general rule. A great many people refused to choose Herbert Hoover over Franklin D. Roosevelt for president of the United States, even though Hoover clearly had more experience with national politics.

We could conceivably treat the criterion of knowledge as no different from the first eight points and dismiss it in these terms. It would be perfectly possible, although not without certain difficulties, to set up a battery of tests that would allow us to separate men in terms of their knowledge. Colleges and universities and the Civil Service Commission do it all the time. We could not, however, demonstrate that men who achieved a certain standard on our test would alone be capable of making the "right" decisions, and any argument of this form would be untenable for the same reasons as the arguments deriving from race or ancestry. But the argument from knowledge as it actually presents itself is much more complex and subtle than this and therefore cannot be disposed of so easily.

Elite rule in the Soviet Union is putatively justified by an argument from knowledge. Rule by Communist Party leadership is proper rule, according to orthodox Communist political philosophy, because that leadership alone possesses clear and accurate knowledge with respect to the proper social, political, and economic goals for society. This, of course, is so because this leadership has been trained in the elaborate metaphysic promulgated by Marx and Engels and perfected by Lenin. But the Marxist-Leninist line will not stand the test of logical scrutiny, as we have shown in detail earlier. Our whole attack on deductive absolutism and our more specific attack on Marx are, of course, extremely relevant here. The important points with respect to this kind of argument have been made, and we

need not repeat them. Above all, what we need to see is that any
political philosophy which attempts to demonstrate the ultimate superiority of a certain decision-making procedure by
deducing it from some account of the way the world *really is*
is fundamentally erroneous. Any such attempt is precisely *irrational*. In the ordinary use of the term, we may be inclined
to think of a Platonic, Hegelian, Marxian, or Thomistic argument as highly *rational* because they are presented in a sophisticated deductive form; but what can "rational" possibly mean
in this context when we have seen that these arguments attempt
to do what cannot be done?

If there is no way of predicting with certitude the consequences of political decisions or of establishing the ultimate
"rightness" of any social goals, then any governmental system
premised on the realization of such possibilities is not and cannot be justified by such premises. So far as my imagination can
stretch, any argument for the ultimate supremacy of elite rule
will be an argument that can be demolished in the way we
have dealt with Lipson's nine. In any case, it seems clear to
me that the *onus probandi* rests with the proponent of elitism.
If someone can show that certain men are to be designated as
rulers by an argument which is not open to the objections we
have here advanced, then we shall be living in a different
world, the human problem will be different, and I shall be
ready to surrender. But this cannot be done in the world
as we know it (or more properly perhaps, do *not* know it),
and we are dealing with a political philosophy for this world.

But if we can direct these arguments against philosophical
proposals of elite rule, can they not similarly be directed
against proposals of majority rule? Indeed they can, *if* the
support advanced for a proposal of majority rule is a matter of
inductive or deductive proof. In sweeping away the alleged
justifications for elite rule, modern philosophers have felt compelled to sweep away justifications for democracy as well, leaving us in a state of overt or disguised relativism. It is again
helpful to look at the problems of political philosophy in terms

of the kinds of controversy that arise in the area. The traditional disputes may be viewed as on three levels, but I suggest that the really important dispute is of a fourth kind. At the first level we can see a dispute between two forms of deductive absolutism. In the modern world the most obvious form of this controversy is that between Catholicism and Communism, between the Vatican and the Kremlin. Both doctrines allege that their political proposals "follow from" *the* correct world view. Thus, a two-layered spiritualist metaphysic opposes a metaphysic of dialectical materialism. A conflict put in these terms seems to me logically unresolvable because, in Stevenson's language, ultimately the conflict is a matter of "attitude."

But there are other thinkers who apparently want to put the Vatican and the Kremlin on the same side and oppose both. This is the second level, which is occupied by Dewey, Popper, and in some ways Weldon. Here the deductive thought model is opposed by the model of inductive "piecemeal engineering," to use Popper's phrase. Piecemeal engineering is all right in a limited context, for example, when proposing a piece of legislation to effect a certain limited end; but it is not satisfactory in matters of ultimate justification. Here enters the third level, which groups the deducers and the inducers on the same side and opposes them with a position of overt relativism. One cannot prove the validity of political proposals by either means and must therefore give up. That we must *not* give up is the force of this entire essay.

What I propose is a fourth level in which we group deducers, inducers, and relativists together, on the grounds that they all conceive of justification as a matter of proof, and that we oppose them with a notion of justification that does not involve proof at all.[10] The justification of democracy *consists in* the rejection of the notion of justification by proof. We have nothing to prove; we have a context in which we must act rationally. It is the very recognition of the fact that one cannot *prove* the validity of political proposals by induction or deduction which leads us to reject any claim to absolute truth, and thereby to reject any political system premised on such a claim. No one man, no group, whether minority or majority, is ever justified in claiming a right to make decisions for the whole society on the grounds that it knows what the "right" decisions are. Just because the "rightness" of a political decision *cannot* be proved—because its consequences, short- or long-range, cannot be predicted with certitude nor its ultimate ethical supremacy demonstrated—are we obligated to construct a decision-making procedure that will leave the way open for new ideas and social change.

Out of the context of man's inability to prove the ultimate validity of political proposals springs the general recommendation that serves as the foundation for political philosophy. Language creaks and strains at the prospect of formulating this recommendation. The problem is to translate the categorical "Be rational" into language appropriate to the context of making political decisions. One hesitates to suggest a phrase, for fear that the inadequacies of the power of expression will cause it to be misinterpreted. For want of better words, I propose these: "Do not block the possibility of change with respect to social goals."

This, however inadequately expressed, is the ultimate "must" of politics. Like Peirce's "Do not block the road to inquiry" *it* cannot be *proved;* but it is absolutely justified unless someone can prove that a certain state of affairs is absolutely "right" and therefore that one is justified in blocking any change. Values for a society might be allocated in an absolutely just way, but we would not be justified in behaving as if they were, for we could not know for sure. To those who suggest the possibility of a universal revelation, whatever this would be like, I can only say that the human problem would then be entirely different; it would be a different world, and the need for political philosophy or for philosophy or science of any kind would dissolve. Philosophy and science exist because of man's ignorance. If perfect knowledge were to be obtained, they would be as useless as a telescope is to God.

Where does our general recommendation take us if our problem consists in setting up a decision-making procedure for a society? This is, of course, the important question; but before we undertake a careful answer, let us take time to reiterate a point to which we have called attention on several earlier occasions. The point referred to is this: it is extremely important to separate the overriding philosophical question of choosing a decision-making procedure *as a matter of principle* from the essentially instrumental questions involved in institutionalizing the principle in an actual political situation. I once heard a distinguished philosopher remark, after a conversation on political theory with a group of political scientists, that the discussion was very difficult because "there were too many questions on the table at once." I think that this is true of much of the writing on democratic theory. Philosophical issues are thrown together with questions of a practical, instrumental character, and the result is often rather muddled. Mixing the questions of ultimate principle with the other questions of representation, communication, responsiveness of leaders, etc., seems to me to hinder clear analysis rather than help it, although any complete theory of democracy will have to deal with such matters. Later we shall examine an important instrumental problem and in this way, I hope, show that by clarifying the philosophical problem first we are able to deal with instrumental matters much more successfully.

I shall begin to discuss the character of the decision-making procedure demanded by our general recommendation in a completely abstract way. I shall pay no attention to the character of the individuals who make up the society, to the physical circumstances in which they live, or to their relations with or relationship to other groups of people. As a practical matter this is, I suspect, impossible; but we shall be blatantly impractical at least for a while. What I am most concerned to achieve for the moment is to temporarily eliminate that knottiest of problems, that of the majority who would destroy democracy. Let us now proceed *in abstracto*.

What does our recommendation "Do not block the possibility of change with respect to social goals" tell us about including or excluding members of the group from the process of decision making for the group? To get at the answer to this question we must look again into the justification for the recommendation. If, as we have suggested, decisions on public policy always involve matters of preference, the ultimate "rightness" of which cannot be demonstrated, then what rational justification can there be for including as a matter of principle the preferences of some while excluding the preferences of others? Any argument that sought to include only the preferences of certain members would be faced with the necessity of demonstrating the ultimate superiority of those preferences or of the people who held them. The argument would thus fall prey to objections that were earlier advanced to elite rule. It is important to note that we are not saying that matters of preference cannot be dealt with at all. One preference is not always or even likely to be just as good as another. Careful analysis and searching argument can clarify and bring agreement about matters of preference in many cases.[11] This is the purpose of legislative debate and political campaigns. But demonstrating the ultimate "rightness" of a policy preference is another matter.

To proceed further, is there any reason to weight the preferences of some more heavily than others as a matter of principle? The answer again must be "no," and the same onerous burden falls upon anyone who wishes to argue that they should. Again this is not to say that some men are not wise and others stupid. There is a good deal of difference between respecting the opinion of the wise and experienced and weighting the vote of some more heavily than others. The former attitude is sensible, but the latter practice is untenable as a matter of principle, if for no other reason than that we have no way of knowing that some men will be wise on all issues and others stupid on all issues.

Is there, at our abstract level, any reason to prevent the expression of any opinion either orally or in writing? Here Peirce's language perhaps makes the point most clearly. If truth is desirable in public policy, then for the reasons already indicated we are never justified in blocking the way of inquiry. To those who wish to argue with Plato that truth is not always desirable in public policy, remember that we are not yet entertaining the preservation of the society as a value. What I am saying here is that on our level of abstraction free expression in its broadest sense is an "absolute"; that is, it should not be restricted in any way.

But decisions *have* to be taken, and if our procedure did not provide a method for taking final and binding decisions, it would fall far short of its purpose. That the majority principle is the only decision-making procedure which comports with the previous dictates of our recommendation has been demonstrated so many times that we need not belabor it here.[12] It is perhaps nowhere more succinctly articulated than by Abraham Lincoln:[13]

> Unanimity is impossible; the rule of a minority as a permanent arrangement, is wholly inadmissible; so that, rejecting the majority principle, anarchy or despotism in some form is all that is left.

Obviously, what we are talking about here are the democratic principles ordinarily denominated "popular sovereignty," "political equality," "individual political rights," and "majority rule." I have talked about them abstractly and have refrained from calling them by name to prevent, as far as possible, tangling with the complexities of their real-world operation, which the labels automatically call to mind. What we have seen here is that our general political recommendation implies the democratic principle, in short, that there is a perfectly rational justification for democracy as a matter of ultimate principle. We have not "deduced" democracy from our recommendation in the formal, logical sense of the term "deduction." It is a good deal more accurate to say that the principles we have enunciated simply *are* the recommendation applied and spelled out. Let us be clear also that the positing of the principles in a certain order does not mean that any are logically prior to others. The principles are justified, so to speak, "all at once," for each is meaningless without the others. To see popular sovereignty, political equality, individual political rights, and majority rule as we have looked at them is to see four aspects of the same general principle. They *all* are the recommendation spelled out—not one, two, or three, to the exclusion of the rest. More than merely compatible with one another, they are necessary to one another. If we are right about this, the arguments belaboring the incompatibility of majority rule and minority rights are on very soft ground.

But let us not get ahead of our story. Let us first of all be sure that we understand what has been accomplished so far. In one sense our major work is done. We set out to examine the logic of democracy and to establish a rational justification for the democratic principle. We promised also to resolve the apparent contradiction between absolutist and relativist approaches to democracy as a philosophical problem. These goals have in essence been reached. We have seen that modern political theory has been caught on the horns of an apparently insoluble dilemma, offering either the misty, metaphysical manipulations of traditional political philosophy or the gnawing discomfort of relativism. But we have, I think, dissolved this dilemma. By seeing in man's fallibility not despair but a rather clear-cut recommendation of what it is rational to do, we are able to support our commitment to democracy not by mere emotion or a vague appeal to the transcendental but by good sense. "The tragedy of Twentieth Century political theory," our inability to defend democracy against totalitarianism, is, as I think we have shown, a tragedy brought about not by any genuine necessity but by a philosophical mistake. Artificially restrictive canons of rationality have brought about the tragedy, and demonstrating that these canons *are* artificial has, I think, removed the tragic effects.

Perhaps the best way of seeing the import of what we have done is to take another look at a statement referred to several times earlier: "We ought to adopt democracy." Without the benefit of the analysis made here, we would probably feel obligated to *prove* the validity of the statement. We would be forced back to "All men are by nature equal" or something like it, a "proposition" which as it stands is anything but self-evident. We would be wide open to positivist attack, and if we were to grant the validity of the attack, we would be driven to the conclusion that the statement "We ought to adopt democracy" expresses the emotional preference of the speaker and little more than this. A political philosophy that expressed such a commitment would have to be considered mere myth, a culturally conditioned response to an environmental stimulus. We would therefore be declared helpless, as far as rationally defending a commitment to democracy is concerned. *But we are not helpless,* as our analysis has shown. Democracy is rationally defensible, and our defense does no violence to scientific standards. We do not say that American or British popular commitment to democracy is not a culturally conditioned response to an environmental stimulus or that "myth" is not a useful concept in social science. There is great insight here, but this is not the whole of it. As a matter of psychology, "We ought to adopt democracy" may on many occasions be equivalent to "Democracy, hurrah!!"; but to say that, as a matter of logic, it is always this way is simply a mistake, and a very disastrous one. We have tried to correct that mistake, and I hope we have in this way cast some light on the problem. A successful justification of democracy, as suggested at the beginning, would have to be capable of convincing anyone with an open mind. I think that the thesis advanced here can sustain this test. I do not suppose that we could convince the oak tree outside my window, and a dedicated Marxist or a monarch who was convinced that Destiny had tapped him on the shoulder might present similar difficulties. To be clearheaded and rational is the best that we can do; to convince people who will not listen is more than can be asked of political philosophy.

What of the apparent paradoxes raised by the absolutism-relativism controversy? As we suggested in our earlier discussion, there is a measure of truth on both sides. Russell is surely right when he says that empiricism is the philosophy which comports with democracy in its "temper of mind." But there is also need and room for a categorical commitment to democracy, as the absolutists have told us. There is, as we have seen, no genuine paradox here but merely an artificial one brought about by equating justification with proof. When we see that at bottom matters of ultimate choice and commitment are not and cannot be questions of proof, the confusion, perplexity, and frustration that accompanied our examination of absolutism and relativism simply fades away. When a commitment to democracy is greeted by a "Prove it," we must reply, "I am sorry, this is just not a matter of proof."

If we have contributed anything to the solution of the philosophical problem of democracy, it has essentially been in the nature of clarification of language. This is just as it should be, for the philosophy of democracy has long been bound up with linguistic confusion. Both empiricism and natural law have been seen as important parts of a philosophy of democracy. These labels and what they imply have led modern investigators to see a necessary choice between the two, on the grounds that maintaining both would be contradictory. Empiricism as ordinarily understood denies the possibility of natural law, and natural law as ordinarily understood denies the validity of empiricism. It is a striking fact that the figure who stands out in the history of political thought as *the* philosopher of democracy held both positions with no apparent compunction. John Locke is perhaps universally recognized as the founder of British empiricism, with his *Essay Concerning Human Understanding* the classic in the field. But he also upholds natural law in the *Second Treatise,* in the recently discovered unpublished essays,[14] and elsewhere. Thus, Locke is often said to

be " . . . full of illogical flaws and inconsistencies."[15] If one
does not go beyond labels, this may be so. However, it has been
argued, and to my mind convincingly, that Locke did not
mean natural law in the classical, deductive sense of the term.[16]
What I suggest here is that Locke was caught up in the language and current of opinion of seventeenth-century England
and could not therefore state the case for democracy as clearly
as it can be stated. What is interesting is that he felt the need
for a categorical commitment to democracy even though he
was quite convinced of man's inability to know the absolute,
and also that he did not see this combination as impossible.
Locke's language probably misled him, and undoubtedly it
has misled subsequent writers on democracy. An elaborate
reinterpretation of Locke would certainly be inappropriate
in the present context, but I do think it worth noting that in
his apparent inconsistency Locke had a better grip on the philosophical justification of democracy than he is sometimes
given credit for. Democracy does involve both an epistemological empiricism (pardon the redundancy) and a categorical
commitment, which in Locke's time could only be expressed
by use of the terms "natural law" or "natural right."

These remarks on Locke lead to another observation that
seems to me worth making. It is unwarranted to denigrate the
American and British tradition of political philosophy on the
grounds that it has produced no great system builders. It
is true enough that the English-speaking nations have produced no Plato, Hegel, or Marx; but in what sense is this
something to be ashamed of? If, as I think we have shown, an
attempt to deduce political proposals from some consummate
"is" is the essence of irrationality and if recognizing man's
intellectual inadequacies is the beginning of wisdom in politics, who comes off better? It seems to me clear that the major
figures in British and American political thought have begun
with just such a recognition and have refused to lose themselves in the labyrinthine reasonings of absolutism. One has
only to get a fair taste of the thinking of Locke, Jefferson, and

John Stuart Mill, as well as Oliver Wendell Holmes, Jr., to
see that whatever their mistakes they were firm supporters of
democracy who had no part of political or philosophical absolutism. They saw the problems of politics in an intensely
practical way, and their convictions with respect to political
freedom were based, in large part at least, upon a recognition
of the limitations of man's knowledge. How much more sensible, how much more rational, are they than their system-
building counterparts elsewhere.

It is not uncommon to hear these men spoken of in rather
patronizing terms because they were involved in practical
affairs. Locke is sometimes called a mere apologist for the
Glorious Revolution; Jefferson and Holmes held high office,
and Mill ran for Parliament. It is quite true that their political
philosophizing was a matter of this world. They did not propose elaborate utopias but tried to give, each in his own way,
sound advice on how to govern in this world. And this is, I
think, a mark of their greatness and their wisdom. This is not
a trait to be disparaged, but one to be praised. I never fail to be
annoyed upon hearing the opinion that the United States and
Great Britain have no adequate tradition in political philosophy. These men and other lesser figures all supported democratic principles and gave more or less good reasons why. Of
course, they proposed no shining social goals dictated by the in-
exorable forces of the universe. They knew better! If one is
concerned to explain why Americans and Britons have very
rarely been seduced by the great ideologies, historical circumstances are surely a factor, but it will not do to leave out the
good, hard thinking exemplified by these writers. If one were
asked to assemble a panel for the purpose of criticizing the
theories of a Marx or a Hegel, could we imagine a better set
of choices than Locke, Jefferson, Mill, and Holmes?

So much for our tradition in political philosophy; there is
little here to be ashamed of. This is a fascinating subject, but
it is a subject for another essay. We have one more point to

make before we look at some of the problems involved in establishing democracy in the real world. The justification for democracy we have proposed is a methodological one, and we are certain to be told that it is *merely* methodological. It might be argued that what we have proposed is merely a justification for democracy as a method of governing; and that this objective misses the point, for the really important thing is "democracy as a way of life." What we have talked about is a mere decision-making procedure, when what is really important is a standard of values that will permeate the whole society. There is a valid point here, but I do not think that we are guilty of missing it. The scope of the recommendation or recommendations based on fallibilism is much broader than the mere establishment of a governing apparatus. The first point to be made is that fallibilism demands an ethic of tolerance apart from any political considerations. If one recognizes the fallibility of his own opinions, it is only consistent to entertain the views of others with a large measure of tolerance. In addition, it seems to me unreasonable to expect a rigid separation between political method and the content of political decision. Professor Henry B. Mayo comments on this point as follows:[17]

> The initial doubt about the virtual neutrality of democracy which arises is this: can any system for political policy-making be strictly neutral or instrumental? In a purely technological sense, we say a tool is merely a tool and may be put to any use, but even here, since some tools are more specialized than others, all tools cannot be put to all uses; and surely democracy, even if "merely a method," must be put in the category of instruments which can only be put to certain uses. Moreover, it seems to be undeniable that the means employed can seldom, if ever, be entirely divorced from the results which actually occur, or which are intended. Means and ends frequently, perhaps always, affect one another, and there is a prima facie case that a complex political system like democracy must have important influences upon the kind of substantive results obtained or aimed at. Concern over procedure is frequently concern over substance, because procedure so often determines the outcome.

Upon reflection it seems clear enough that the justification of method also involves the justification of certain results. I would not know how to go about justifying in some ultimate sense the equalization of wealth in a society except by saying we are obligated to set up a procedure for decision making that will give the widest opportunity for popular preference. I see no reason for saying that nature dictates a high standard of living for all men, for nature has certainly given us very little evidence in support of this thesis. I do, however, see a very good reason for denying Herbert Spencer's dictum that the wealthy are wealthy and the poor are poor because of their respective virtues. Who will deny that the actualization of political equality through extension of suffrage rebutted Mr. Spencer as nothing else could have?

The evidence for the complimentarity of a democratic decision-making procedure and the values associated with the concept of "democracy as a way of life" is very great. Democracy as a set of popular values and democracy as a decision-making procedure reinforce one another at every turn. Adherence to notions of political equality leads, perhaps inevitably, to demands for social and economic equality; and greater social and economic equality in turn makes political equality more genuine. Justice Frankfurter's famous remark, "The history of liberty has largely been the history of observance of procedural safeguards," in one way testifies to the intimate relationship between method and substance. The researches of modern social science have shown us that, in nations where political democracy is well established, democratic values are rooted deeply in popular social practice.[18] To justify a decision-making procedure as we have done it cannot, I think, be regarded as merely methodological. It says a good deal about the "substantive" values that men should hold as well. Any careful examination of ethics will surely show that there is no clear-cut distinction between means and ends, between what is done and how it is done—that is, between method and substance.

NOTES

[1] Albert Camus, *The Rebel* (New York: Alfred A. Knopf, Inc., 1956), p. 3.

[2] Isaiah Berlin, *Two Concepts of Liberty* (New York: Oxford University Press, 1958), p. 4.

[3] Cf. James Ward Smith, *Theme for Reason* (Princeton, N.J.: Princeton University Press, 1957), pp. 29–30.

[4] Camus, *op. cit.*, p. 4.

[5] David Easton, *The Political System* (New York: Alfred A. Knopf, Inc., 1953), p. 129.

[6] I mean "decision-making procedure" in the sense of "type of government," not in any of its more restricted usages.

[7] Cf. Easton, *op. cit.*, pp. 129–130.

[8] C. L. Stevenson, *Ethics and Language* (New Haven, Conn.: Yale University Press, 1944), p. 11. (Italics in original.)

[9] Leslie Lipson, *The Great Issues of Politics: An Introduction to Political Science.* © 1960, 2nd ed., Prentice-Hall, Inc., p. 95.

[10] Cf. Smith, *op. cit.*, pp. 109–110.

[11] See Stephen Edelston Toulmin, *An Examination of the Place of Reason in Ethics* (New York: Cambridge University Press, 1953); and Stevenson, *op. cit.*

[12] See, for example, Austin Ranney and Willmoore Kendall, *Democracy and the American Party System* (New York: Harcourt, Brace & World, Inc., 1956), pp. 29–39; Henry B. Mayo, *An Introduction to Democratic Theory* (New York: Oxford University Press, 1960), p. 178; and the symbolic demonstration in Robert A. Dahl, *A Preface to Democratic Theory.* Copyright 1956 by the University of Chicago. (Chicago: University of Chicago Press), pp. 60–61.

[13] Quoted in Mayo, *op. cit.*, p. 179.

[14] John Locke, *Essays on the Law of Nature,* ed. by W. von Leyden (Oxford: Clarendon Press, 1954).

[15] J. W. Gough, *John Locke's Political Philosophy* (New York: Oxford University Press, 1950), p. 123.

[16] Leo Strauss, *Natural Right and History.* Copyright 1953 by the University of Chicago. (Chicago: University of Chicago Press).

[17] Mayo, *op. cit.*, p. 214.

[18] See Zevedei Barbu, *Democracy and Dictatorship: Their Psychology and Patterns of Life* (New York: Grove Press, Inc., 1956), pp. 93–105. David B. Truman calls attention repeatedly to adherence to "rules of the game" as characteristic of democratic society, proceeding in large part from the essentially methodological character of democracy. *The Governmental Process* (New York: Alfred A. Knopf, Inc., 1955).

9

MAJORITY RULE AND MINORITY RIGHTS

We have, up to this point, been very careful to avoid the problem that most democratic theorists would regard as the most difficult and most important one. The problem arises because of the ever-present possibility under a democratic governmental structure that the right of the majority to rule will come into conflict with the right of individuals and minorities to assert and register in a formal way their political preferences. If, as most democrats in the Western political tradition would admit, democracy necessarily involves the application and utilization of both the principle of majority rule and the principle of minority rights, the potential conflicts can be placed in two broad categories. The first of these is majority action that deprives a minority of its legitimate role in the democratic decision-making process (e.g., by denying free expression or suffrage). The second is action on the part of a minority that deprives a majority of the legitimate right to rule (e.g., the abuse of the power of judicial review by the United States Supreme Court). This problem in its manifold aspects is one which will be quite familiar to anyone who has had contact with democratic government.

The argument I wish to make in this final chapter is that the role of the political philosopher in dealing with this problem has been vastly overestimated. I do not think that it is legitimately a philosophical problem or even, in one sense of the term, legitimately a theoretical problem. By this I mean that the political philosopher *qua* political philosopher cannot solve it. He *can,* however—and this is quite important— show why it cannot be solved by philosophical means and thus clarify the *nature* of the solution.

There is no single theoretical solution to the problem of majority rule and minority rights; rather, there are solutions of various kinds, the choice of which turns upon the gathering of relevant empirical evidence. The opinion is nonetheless widespread that this is a problem susceptible of theoretical solution. It has in fact been called by reputable authority "the greatest single theoretical controversy about the nature of democracy."[1] That this essentially empirical question should be seen as a theoretical question is, I think, the result of faulty philosophizing.

In one sense, there is an almost infinite variety of writers about democracy, each in one respect or another looking at democracy in a slightly different perspective. However, as was suggested before, so far as the majority rule–minority rights question is concerned, there are two major categories. On the one hand, there are those who see democracy essentially as an instrument for limiting the powers of governmental officials. For them the widest possible freedom for individuals consistent with stable government is the highest value. What they fear most of all is tyranny, and often the sort of tyranny most feared is the tyranny of the majority.[2] To this camp belong the most notable figures in early American democratic thought: surely James Madison, in some measure Thomas Jefferson, and certainly John C. Calhoun. Typically, the philosophical point of departure for democrats of this school is some sort of conception of the natural rights of men. Let us then lump them together under the general rubric "natural rights democrats."[3]

The contrary view, which is generally speaking the more modern one, sees democracy as the method of popular government. The stress here is laid upon popular sovereignty, political equality, and therefore upon majority rule. The test of whether a governmental act is democratic or not is not so much a matter of how it affects individuals as it is of whether the policy has been decided upon by a majority of the citizenry. There is less emphasis upon limiting governmental activity and more emphasis upon allowing the majority to do what it wants. It seems fair to say that this view of democracy is held by jurists such as Felix Frankfurter and Learned Hand and by political scientists such as Austin Ranney and Willmoore Kendall. Such a position can be and has been worked out in a variety of ways. Generally implicit and often explicit in the view, however, is a denial of the possibility of knowing natural law and natural rights and the consequent conclusion that the will of the majority is the only ultimate test in politics. Frankfurter, for example, has had occasion to refer to the Supreme Court as "non-democratic" and "inherently oligarchic,"[4] thus implying that for him majority rule is the prime element in democracy. Similarly, a close reading of the Ranney and Kendall model of an "ideally democratic government" reveals majority rule to be the crucial element.[5] These are what we may fairly call "majority rule democrats."

We need to be clear that the difference between "natural rights democrats" and "majority rule democrats," to which I have attempted to call attention, is less a matter of wholly contradictory notions of democracy than a matter of different theoretical casts of mind. All democrats will recognize the need for both majority rule and the protection of minority rights. The difference is a matter of emphasis. As Robert A. Dahl has stated it,[6]

> . . . so far as I am aware, no one has ever advocated, and no one except its enemies has ever defined democracy to mean, that a majority would or should do anything it felt an impulse to do. Every advocate of democracy of whom I am aware, and every friendly definition of it, includes the idea of restraints on majorities. But one central issue is whether these restraints are, or should be, (1) primarily internalized restraints in the individual behavior system, such as the conscience and other products of social indoctrination, (2) primarily social checks and balances of several kinds, or (3) primarily prescribed constitutional checks. Among political systems to which the term "democracy" is commonly applied in the Western world, one important difference is between those which rely primarily on the first two checks, and those like the United States which also employ constitutional checks.

Because of the existence of constitutional checks in the United States, controversy over the proper roles of majority rule and minority rights has flourished among Americans. The questions to confront in this connection are two: (A) Should there be constitutional checks at all? (B) Given that constitutional checks exist, how should they be applied?

The affirmative answer to question A classically takes the following form:

1. All men are endowed with certain natural rights. Among these are life, liberty, property, and the pursuit of happiness.
2. The severe deprivation of these natural rights is tyranny.
3. The true or proper purpose of government is the protection of these rights or, to say the same thing another way, the prevention of tyranny.
4. Minorities can be prevented from depriving other members of the society of their natural rights by the operation of the principle of majority rule.
5. Majorities can be prevented from depriving other members of the society of their natural rights by the operation of constitutional checks on their power.
6. Therefore, constitutional checks on the power of majorities should be employed.

There is no need to elaborate the roles of Locke, Madison, Jefferson, and Calhoun in promoting one or another aspect of this view. Considered historically, this argument represents the mainstream of American democratic thought.

One can object to the argument in a number of ways. Professor Dahl, for example, is willing in terms of his analysis to grant the natural rights premise but seeks to demonstrate, quite successfully, that the requirement of constitutional checks does not follow on empirical grounds.[7] My quarrel is with the natural rights premise itself. The conception of democracy presented in this argument quite clearly makes natural rights the prime principle and majority rule a secondary one. For this reason its adherents were not content with social and cultural checks upon the power of majorities but demanded constitutional checks as well. Thus, Dahl's argument that constitutional checks do not *necessarily* follow from the premises, while completely accurate as far as it goes, in a certain sense misses a point of great significance. What, most fundamentally, is wrong with this argument is that it identifies the justification of democracy with the justification of natural rights.

The man who sees the protection of natural rights as the very definition of democracy does not need a conclusive demonstration of the necessity of constitutional checks on majorities. For him the likelihood that they will help is enough. But his definition is wrong, because it presumes the existence of a set of qualities or properties that attach to each man. The existence of these qualities or properties is supposedly proved by observation and inductive generalization, or by deductive demonstration from some grand principle—"These truths are self-evident," "All men are endowed with reason," "All men are created in the image of God." We have, I trust, said enough about these lines of argument.

Do not misunderstand my point. My argument is not against constitutional checks on majorities, nor does it suggest that there are no human rights which should be protected. Rather, my contention is that the conception of democracy which holds natural rights to be the prime principle is faulty because it seeks to justify by proof when no proof is possible. When the argument for constitutional checks is contingent upon such proof as it is in the classical argument, it is also faulty.

The contrary theoretical solution to the problem of constitutional checks posed by question A is equally invalid. This position demands, in the words of Professors Ranney and Kendall, that no *"formal* institutional limitations" be placed on the power of popular majorities. This conclusion is said to follow from the definition of democracy in the following way:[8]

1. Political equality and popular sovereignty are principles of democracy.
2. Majority rule alone is compatible with these principles. (Minority rule is incompatible with political equality and popular sovereignty because it violates them by definition, and unanimity is impossible.)
3. Any attempt at formal institutional limitation (e.g., a Supreme Court with the power of judicial review, the requirements for extraordinary majorities) necessarily involves minority rule.
4. Ergo, no formal institutional limitations on the power of majorities are legitimate from a democratic point of view.

This argument seeks by an exercise of "strict logic," as Ranney and Kendall say several times, to solve the problem of constitutional checks by deduction from the basic democratic premises. Again, it may be criticized from several angles. First of all, the conclusion quite simply does not follow from the premises. The conclusion—*no* formal institutional limitations on the power of popular majorities—is too broad. It is quite reasonable to say that, with respect to a wide range of social policy choices, only majority rule is the legitimate democratic principle because of its compatibility with political equality and popular sovereignty. On the other hand, it is hardly reasonable to argue that with respect to majority actions which abrogate political equality and popular sovereignty (e.g., denial of suffrage, free expression, or the opportunity to run for public office) majority rule alone is legitimate because of its compatibility with political equality and popular sovereignty. But this is what the conclusion "*no* constitutional checks" must mean, if it means anything at all. Thus, as an exercise in "strict logic" the argument is a failure.[9]

Because this argument is in large part a modern one, advanced in an era dominated by an empiricist-positivist *Weltanschauung*, questions of philosophical justification are not often explicitly raised in connection with it. Ranney and Kendall, for example, do not explicitly attempt to justify political equality or popular sovereignty; rather, these principles are given. "No one thinks of democracy" without thinking of these two principles.[10] I suspect quite strongly, however, that the implicit justification of the argument is at the core of its inadequacy.

While this argument usually goes by the name "absolute majority rule," it might more precisely be described as absolute "antiminority" rule. The case *for* majority rule is developed wholly from the case *against* minority rule. Here are Ranney and Kendall on this point:[11]

> A policy or procedure, obviously, does not gain in rightness by picking up enough support to justify the claim that it represents the wishes of a majority, or lose in rightness by losing support. But that is not the point at issue, since what the majoritarian asserts is not the superior intelligence or wisdom or even morality of popular majorities, but the wrongness, from the democratic point of view, of a state of affairs where the few are in a position to have their way over the wishes of the many.

But what *is* wrong with minority rule? The immediate answer would surely be that "it violates political equality and popular sovereignty." But why these principles? My guess is that the answer we would get to this question, and therefore the real answer to the first question, would be a truncated version of the argument from fallibilism. The reasoning would probably be something like this:

1. No man (or group of men) can demonstrate the rightness of his preferences.
2. Therefore, all men must be treated as equal and allowed to rule.
3. Therefore, no minority should be allowed to rule.
4. If not minority rule, then majority rule.

But this argument *is* truncated; it is oversimplified. Fallibilism prescribes no such simple numerical rule but a general directive on leaving the way open for a change in social goals.

The so-called "absolute majority rule" argument eliminates the majority rule–minority rights problem by deductive fiat; and as we have seen, the deduction is faulty.

The conclusion to be drawn from all this is that the controversy over constitutional checks is not to be resolved in either direction by abstract reasoning. The decision to have constitutional checks or not to have them can only turn on an estimate of the empirical situation. The categorical of fallibilism demands that the way be kept open for a change in goals. The categorical, as we have seen, implies the maximization of political equality, popular sovereignty, minority political rights, and majority rule. When faced with the problem of actually designing real-world institutions, this ideal procedure is (or should be) a prime value; but the preservation and stability of the society is also a value. The choice between giving majorities free rein or constitutionally checking them can be sensibly made only by assessing the relative costs of the alternatives. Who in this particular society is more likely to abuse power, a majority or a minority? This is the question, and clearly it is an empirical question, not a theoretical or philosophical one.

Treating the majority rule–minority rights problem as essentially resolved by either a natural rights argument or an "absolute majority rule" argument can lead to very important practical consequences. A good deal of American constitutional history can be understood in these terms. It would be beyond the scope of this essay to discuss this history in any detail. Let me instead discuss a hypothetical society, which I suspect will nonetheless sound a bit familiar. This discussion will deal with question B: given that constitutional checks exist, how should they be applied?

Imagine a society with a democratic governmental structure. This democratic structure is provided for in a written constitution that is to be the supreme law of society. To the legislature and the executive is given a general grant of power to promote the general welfare. The legislature and the executive are specifically prohibited from abridging free expression, suffrage, the right to run for public office, and the right peaceably to assemble. The legislature and the executive are also prohibited from expropriating private property without due process of law. A supreme judicial body with the power of judicial review is also provided for. The constitution is very difficult to amend, so that the exercise of the power of judicial review is quite effective.

This is clearly a constitutional-check situation. The supreme judicial body, a minority, is given the power to check the action of majorities. The delegation of this power is anything but clear. When does a legislative act promote the general welfare, and when is it deleterious to the general welfare? What are the limits on free expression? What is a peaceful assembly? What is due process of law? All these questions will require answers from the members of the supreme judicial body, and it is clear that a mere reading of the constitution, no matter how assiduous, cannot provide them. The judges will therefore have to define their role in this democratic process which the constitution attempts to create. How the judges do this will surely in part turn on their conceptions of democracy. Undoubtedly the formation of attitudes on these questions will be the result of a wide variety of environmental factors, including presumably socioeconomic class origins, experience prior to appointment, and education. A particular judge's conception of democracy will be here created and there reinforced by these factors, but he is likely to have a conception of democracy at the level of articulation.

Suppose a majority of judges share a natural rights conception of democracy and see democratic government basically as limited government. How are these judges likely to react to cases that involve a conflict between the wishes of the majority as reflected by the legislature and the freedom to act of individuals affected by the statute in question? Surely it would not be surprising to find them using their power of judicial review aggressively—striking down what they consider to be majority infringement on the freedom of individuals. For these judges "the general welfare" would likely be defined in terms of the freedom to act of individuals. For them "due process of law" might come to mean not only a set of regular procedures but also a substantive directive with regard to the wisdom of certain policies. That this conception of democracy might lead to a frustration of majority desires, to a blocking of the possibility of change with respect to social goals, appears rather clear. That statutes limiting child labor, fixing maximum hours and minimum wages, or coercing payment for old-age pensions might be struck down as infringing freedom of contract or as deleterious to the general welfare would not be surprising.

Suppose, on the other hand, that the court majority held a majority rule conception of democracy. Would not this majority be likely to regard its whole position as somewhat tenuous? Might not judges holding this view see the judicial body of which they were a part as "non-democratic" and "inherently oligarchic," to use words written by Mr. Justice Frankfurter in a not dissimilar context. Majority rule democrats on the court might adopt, as the rule of behavior with respect to the use of the power of judicial review, not the aggressiveness of the natural rights democrats but a doctrine of self-restraint toward the preferences of majorities.

If the legislature were to adopt a statute limiting the right to speak and write of a group of social, political, or economic heretics, a judge who held majority rule to be the very definition of democracy might be quite reluctant to employ judicial review against it. If free expression is limited by a frightened and myopic majority, the possibility of changing social goals is blocked to that extent.

My line of argument, I hope, is now clear. Conceptions of democracy, justifications of democracy that elevate either natural rights or the principle of majority rule to a position of primacy, can lead to practical consequences of great importance. We have tried to show that such justifications are faulty, and we call instead for a conception of democracy which makes no institutional principle supreme but which holds that the principles are mutually interdependent and essentially equal. They are the spelling out of the general categorical recommendation "Be rational" when setting up a political system. According to this view, it is quite consistent for judges empowered with judicial review to be self-restrained in the face of majority preferences on general social policy *and* to be aggressive in the use of their power when free expression, suffrage, or the right to run for public office is in question. Thus, thinking through the logic of democracy can be of great importance to actors in the democratic process.

There is no suggestion here that all the problems involved in implementing democracy will be magically solved if "the proper" justification of democracy is adopted. The categorical of rationality is no Euclidean theorem from which the answers to all problems follow by demonstration. Empirical concerns, or matters of fact, are crucial to every political problem; but matters of choice are equally crucial. One of the functions of the political scientist, the economist, the sociologist, the psychologist, and the anthropologist is to find and present the facts relevant to these problems.

The political philosopher, on the contrary, is not a superscientist. The definition of his task does not include the possession of a superior insight into the way the world *is*. He tries instead to think through matters of choice, often of ultimate choice, for citizens who have not the time or resources to do it for themselves. Unless one is willing to adopt the metaphysic that human beings are Pavlovian dogs whose behavior is *entirely* to be understood as a set of responses to irrational stimuli, this is a task of greatest importance, and it should not be rejected because political philosophers have at times been far too pretentious or because they have made mistakes. Political philosophy can be good or bad, helpful or useless. If it is wrong, it should be criticized, but it should be criticized in its own terms. It is recommendation, not fact. To criticize political philosophy because it is not fact is no criticism at all. Like all political philosophers, Plato made many mistakes, but he made no mistake when he cast the first political philosophy in the form of a dialogue. Mistakes call for criticism, and if he understands his role, the political philosopher welcomes them.

NOTES

1 Austin Ranney and Willmoore Kendall, *Democracy and the American Party System* (New York: Harcourt, Brace & World, Inc., 1956), p. 29.

2 Cf. Robert A. Dahl, *A Preface to Democratic Theory*. Copyright 1956 by the University of Chicago. (Chicago: University of Chicago Press), pp. 4–33.

3 This categorization compares in large measure with Professor Dahl's notion of Madisonian democracy. *Ibid.*

4 *AFL v. American Sash and Door Co.*, 335 U.S. 538 (1949), 555.

5 Ranney and Kendall, *op. cit.*, pp. 1–82.

6 Dahl, *op. cit.*, p. 36.

7 *Ibid.*, pp. 11–15.

8 "*Why 'Absolute' Majority Rule?* For the reasons given in the foregoing pages, any attempt to place *formal* institutional limitations upon the 'absolute' power of popular majorities logically results in the establishment of *minority* rule. And from the standpoint of logic, 'absolute' majority rule must be chosen over minority rule as a principle of ideally democratic government, not because there is any magical or omniscience in popular majorities, but because majority rule is more nearly in accord than minority rule with the other principles of democracy that we have previously discussed." Ranney and Kendall, *op. cit.*, pp. 29–37. (Italics in original.)

9 See Thomas Landon Thorson, "Epilogue on Absolute Majority Rule," *The Journal of Politics*, vol. XXIII (August, 1961), pp. 557–565.

10 Ranney and Kendall, *op. cit.*, p. 29.

11 *Ibid.*, p. 32.